# STEP AWAY FROM THE KEYBOARD, KEVIN

COYOTE GRAY JR

Published by Coyote Pack Publishing

Artwork and cover design by Coyote Gray III

ISBN: 978-1-972671-10-8

Printed in the United States of America

First Edition

This book is a work of nonfiction. Kevin is a pattern. Any resemblance to Kevin is not coincidental. *You know what you did.* Kevin is a person who believes effort should replace talent, and visibility should replace judgment.

The publisher assumes no liability for damaged writing groups, terminated accountability partnerships, deleted Scrivener files, dissolved MFA cohorts, unfollowed craft accounts, or the sudden and overdue burial of manuscripts that deserved it.

If you are reading this page instead of writing, the diagnosis has already begun.

No Kevins were consulted in the making of this book. Several were observed. One submitted a query letter during the research phase. It was not requested. It was not ready. It was very long.

Sorting is not cruelty. This page is not an exception.

You can stop reading this and go back to what you were doing at any time.

*For Sam Kinison*
*You screamed it first.*
*Nobody listened then either.*
***AHHHHHHHHHHHHH!!!!***

# CONTENTS

**Kevin** (*n.*) ˈkɛv.ɪn

    1 A person of any gender who believes effort entitles them to recognition.

    2 A writer who mistakes activity for skill and persistence for talent.

    3 A creative who has produced at least one manuscript and approximately zero evidence of improvement.

*The Kevin believes effort should replace talent, and visibility should replace judgment.*

See also: Sunk Cost Fallacy; Vanity Press; Local Legend Syndrome.

# AUTHOR'S NOTE

This book is a polemical intervention. It diagnoses a pattern, and it forces a choice. It does both on purpose.

Nothing here is craft instruction. Nothing here is therapy. Nothing here is encouragement. Nothing here is reform.

This book gives no steps, no systems, no exercises, no tools, and no "five things successful writers do differently". It issues verdicts. It names patterns. It forces choices. The choices are two: finish or stop. The book has no third option to sell you.

Descriptions are diagnostic. The patterns are named because they recur. Recognition is the intended effect.

Identity grants no exemption here. Pain grants no authority here. Effort grants no verdict here. Intention grants no outcome here.

Only artifacts are evaluated. Only readers decide. Only endings deliver the verdict.

Sorting is not cruelty. Silence is not injustice. Alignment is not failure.

Some dreams deserve to die. This book will tell you if yours is one of them.

It will not apologize for telling you.

**Tone Calibration:**

This book is what happens when Sam Kinison reads _The Elephant in the Brain_, slams it shut halfway through, and screams:

**"NO. NO. NO! WE'RE NOT PETTING THE ELEPHANT. WE'RE STRAPPING DYNAMITE TO IT."**

_**Proceed accordingly.**_

# CHAPTER ONE
## THE LION'S DEN

**THE LION IS NOT ANGRY. THE LION IS WAITING.**

STOP.

Put down the laptop. Close the Scrivener file. Step away from the coffee shop table where you have been performing concentration for an audience of strangers who do not care.

You are not a writer.

You are a person who has confused the warmth of intention with the cold fact of output. You have mistaken the announcement for the act.

You have told everyone who would listen, and several who would not, that you are "working on something." You have said the word "novel" in public, tasted how it felt in your mouth, and decided that the taste was enough.

It is not enough.

There is a difference between a writer and a person who likes the idea of being a writer. The difference is not talent. The difference is not time. The difference is not opportunity, access, privilege, or luck.

The difference is a finished manuscript that someone who does not love you can hold in their hands and judge without mercy.

You do not have that.

You have announcements.

You have intentions.

You have a folder on your desktop called "NOVEL" that contains six abandoned first chapters, a character sheet for a protagonist who will never breathe, and a playlist you made to capture the "vibe" of a story that does not exist.

The playlist is longer than the manuscript.

This is not writer's block.

Writer's block is what happens when a writer has written themselves into a corner. You have not written yourself into anything. You are standing in an empty room, admiring the architecture of the walls you have not built, and calling it a house.

You have told your mother.

She said it sounded wonderful.

She said she was proud of you.

She said she could not wait to read it.

She will wait forever.

Her waiting will never become impatience, because her love is unconditional and therefore diagnostically worthless.

Her pride is not data. Her encouragement is not evidence. Her belief in you is not the market.

The market is something else entirely.

**The market is a lion.**

It is old and vast and utterly indifferent to your struggle. It does not care how long you have been working. It does not care how much you have sacrificed. It does not care about your childhood trauma, your unique perspective, or your voice that sounds like no one else's voice.

The lion has heard ten thousand voices that sounded like no one else's voice. They all sounded the same.

The lion wants one thing only: to be held.

Not impressed.

Not intrigued.

Not shown potential.

**Held.**

A sentence that grips. A paragraph that refuses to release. A page that earns the next page. A book that makes a stranger, someone with no obligation to you, someone who paid money and spent hours, feel that the money and hours were well spent.

That is the only verdict that matters.

Everything else is noise.

You walk into the lion's den carrying your three chapters and your "unique voice." You are strumming a ukulele. You have practiced the ukulele in your bedroom for two years. You have told everyone you are a musician. You have purchased a special case for the ukulele. You have taken photographs of yourself holding the ukulele and posted them with captions about your "creative journey."

The lion does not hear music.

The lion hears noise.

Small noise.

The noise of someone who has never performed for an audience capable of leaving.

The noise of someone who has only ever played for rooms that were required to clap.

The lion does not clap.

The lion yawns.

The lion waits.

The lion, eventually, eats.

And when the lion eats your dream, when the query letters vanish into silence, when the agents do not reply, when the small press folds before your book sees print, when the sales numbers arrive and they are a number so small it could be a family reunion, when the reviews do not come because no one cared enough to have an opinion, when the silence stretches out like a corpse and you realize that no one is coming to save you, no one is coming to discover you, no one is coming at all...

You will not blame the work.

The work is sacred. The work is you. To blame the work would be to admit that the work was not good enough, and if the work was not good enough, then the two years were wasted, and if the two years were wasted, then you are not who you said you were.

That is unbearable.

So you will blame something else.

The algorithm is broken. The gatekeepers are corrupt. Publishing is a dying industry run by cowards. Readers have no taste. The market is rigged against new voices. Amazon is a monopoly. BookTok is a lottery. Luck is the only variable, and you were unlucky.

You will tell this story until you believe it. You will find others who believe it too. You will gather in forums and comment sections and writing groups where everyone agrees that the system is unfair and the cream does not rise and talent is unrecognized and persistence is punished and the only thing standing between you and success is a world that refuses to see what you have to offer.

**You will become Kevin.**

Kevin is not a person.

Kevin is a pattern.

Kevin is what happens when the absence of evidence meets the refusal to stop.

Kevin is the noise that fills the void where a verdict should be.

Kevin is the writer who has never finished, the musician who has never performed, the entrepreneur who has never shipped, the artist who has never sold, who nonetheless demands to be treated as though finishing, performing, shipping, and selling are irrelevant details beneath the dignity of a true creative.

Kevin culture teaches that effort is achievement. That intention is execution. That announcing is the same as doing, and being on the journey is the same as arriving.

Kevin culture is wrong.

Effort is the entry fee. Millions of people pay it. Effort is what gets you to the door. It is not what gets you through. What gets you through is an artifact that holds, and most people, most of the time, do not produce artifacts that hold.

This is not tragedy.

This is arithmetic.

Some people cannot sing. Some people cannot paint. Some people cannot write prose that a stranger would pay money and hours to experience.

This is not cruelty. This is the distribution of ability in a species of eight billion. Someone has to be average. Someone has to be below average. Someone has to be significantly below average but convinced they are significantly above.

That someone might be you.

This book will not tell you otherwise. This book will not reassure you that your dream is valid. This book will not offer a path, a method, a framework, a set of exercises to unlock your potential.

This book does not believe in your potential. This book believes in your output, and your output does not yet exist in a form that can be judged.

When it does, the lion will judge it.

Until then, you are noise.

This book is a diagnostic. It names a pattern you may recognize. If you recognize the pattern in someone else, congratulations. If you recognize the pattern in yourself, this is the moment the book begins to work.

Some dreams deserve to die.

Not all dreams. Not most dreams. But some.

The dreams that have calcified into identity. The dreams that demand protection from reality. The dreams that have become too precious to expose to a verdict.

Those dreams are tumors. They grow by consuming the tissue around them: time, money, relationships, sanity. They survive by convincing their host that removal would be fatal.

Removal is not fatal. Removal is the surgery that lets you live.

But no one is going to perform that surgery for you. Not your mother. Not your writing group. Not your followers. Not this book.

This book strips away excuses. That is all it does. It does

not provide comfort. It does not provide direction. It does not provide hope.

It names the pattern, burns the hiding places, and leaves you standing in the open with nothing between you and the lion but whatever you have actually made.

If you have made something that holds, the lion will not eat you.

If you have not, the lion does not owe you a second chance.

Some dreams deserve to die.

Yours might be one of them.

If this offends you into action, the pattern was real.

If this offends you into argument, the pattern is terminal.

The lion is waiting.


***Now get through the door, or get out of the way.***

# CHAPTER TWO
## THE DECLARATION

**The costume arrived before the evidence**

IT ALWAYS BEGINS the same way.

Someone opens their mouth at a party, a family dinner, a first date, a work event, and says the words:

*"I'm writing a book."*

Not "I wrote a book." Not "Here it is." Not "Judge it."

Just: "I'm writing."

Present tense.

Infinite.

A flag planted in territory that has not been conquered. You have claimed a kingdom that does not exist.

**The Declaration.**

Watch what happens next. Watch the face of the person who made it. Watch how they hold themselves in the seconds after the words leave their mouth.

There is a shift. A straightening. A subtle inflation, as though the sentence itself pumped air into their posture.

They have said the magic words. They have claimed the identity. They are now, in their own mind and in the social record of this conversation, a **Writer**.

No pages were required. No manuscript was produced. No artifact was submitted to judgment. The identity was claimed by declaration alone, and the declaration was accepted because no one at a party, a family dinner, a first date, or a work event is going to ask the follow up question that would collapse the whole performance:

*"Can I read it?"*

That question is rude. That question is unsupportive. That question implies doubt, and doubt is violence, and violence against a creative person's dream is the kind of cruelty that polite society has learned to avoid.

So no one asks. The declaration stands. The Writer walks away with their new identity intact, wrapped around them like a coat they have not paid for.

This is the first lie.

Not a lie told to others.

A lie told to the self.

The lie that saying is the same as doing.

The lie that intention is execution.

The lie that the distance between "I want to write a

book" and "I have written a book" is measured in time rather than in work.

Time does not write books.

Work writes books.

Thousands of hours of showing up when you do not want to. Thousands of decisions made in sequence, each one narrowing the infinite possibility of the blank page into the specific, flawed, vulnerable reality of a sentence that can be read by someone who does not love you.

The Declaration skips all of that. The Declaration takes the destination and pastes it over the journey. The Declaration says: *I am already there. I have already arrived. The only thing missing is the artifact, and the artifact is a detail, a technicality, a formality that will be handled eventually, someday, when the time is right.*

**The time is never right.**

The time is never right because finishing is terrifying. Finishing means the thing you made can be seen. Finishing means the thing you made can be judged. Finishing means the end of potential and the beginning of verdict.

Potential is infinite. Potential cannot be killed. As long as the book remains unwritten, it could be anything. It could be the great American novel. It could be a bestseller. It could change lives, win awards, silence the doubters, vindicate every choice you have ever made.

The unwritten book is perfect because it does not exist, and things that do not exist cannot disappoint.

The written book is a corpse.

The written book has a shape, a length, a beginning and an end. The written book has sentences that could have been better and chapters that drag and a third act that does not quite land. The written book can be rejected by agents, dismissed by publishers, ignored by readers, savaged by reviewers.

The written book can fail. The written book can prove that you are not who you said you were.

So Kevin never writes the book.

Kevin writes the first chapter. Kevin writes the first chapter several times, in fact, because the first chapter is the part that feels like writing without being writing. The first chapter is all setup, all promise, all potential. The first chapter does not require Kevin to make the hard decisions that come later: what happens, why it matters, how it ends. The first chapter lets Kevin feel like a writer without demanding that Kevin become one.

Then something interrupts. Life gets busy. Work gets stressful. The idea needs more research. The outline is not quite right. A better idea arrives, shinier than the last, and Kevin pivots. Kevin starts a new first chapter for a new book that will also never be finished, and the cycle begins again.

Three years pass. Kevin has written six first chapters for six different books. Kevin has finished nothing. Kevin has published nothing. Kevin has submitted nothing to the judgment of strangers.

But Kevin is still a Writer.

Kevin knows this because Kevin declared it, and the declaration was never challenged. Kevin's mother asks about the book at every holiday, and Kevin says it is "coming along." Kevin's friends have learned not to ask too many questions, because the questions make Kevin defensive, and defensive Kevin is unpleasant to be around. Kevin's social media bio says "Author" or "Writer" or "Storyteller" or some other word that claims the identity without providing the evidence.

The identity is everything. The identity is what Kevin

was after from the beginning. The book was never the point. The book was the excuse for the identity, and the identity has been successfully claimed, so the book is no longer necessary.

This is what Kevin cannot admit.

Kevin cannot admit that the goal was never the artifact. The goal was the feeling of being a person who creates artifacts. The goal was the social status, the internal narrative, the story Kevin tells about Kevin. The book was a prop in that story, and props do not need to be real. They only need to be believed.

But the belief is fragile.

The belief requires maintenance.

The belief requires Kevin to keep saying "I'm writing a book" at parties, family dinners, first dates, and work events.

The belief requires Kevin to keep posting about "the creative process" and "the journey" and "the struggle."

The belief requires Kevin to surround himself with other people who are also Declaring, so that Declaration becomes normalized, so that the absence of artifacts is never mentioned because everyone in the room is equally absent.

This is how **Kevin Culture** reproduces.

Kevin finds other Kevins.

They form writing groups. They meet weekly to discuss their *works in progress*, which are always in progress and never finished. They share their first chapters. They praise each other's first chapters. They say things like "this has so much potential" and "I can't wait to read more" and "you really have something here."

They create an economy of encouragement in which the currency is enthusiasm and the product is permission to continue without producing.

No one in the group has published a book.

No one in the group will publish a book.

But everyone in the group is a Writer, because they have all Declared, and they have all accepted each other's Declarations, and that mutual acceptance has created a reality in which the Declaration is sufficient.

Outside the group, the lion waits.

Outside the group, there are people who have finished books. People who have submitted books. People who have been rejected and revised and rejected again and kept going because the identity was not the point, the artifact was the point, and the artifact was not going to build itself.

Those people do not talk about their "creative journey." Those people do not post about their "process." Those people sit in rooms alone and do the work because the work is the only thing that produces the object that can be judged.

Kevin hates those people.

Kevin does not say this directly. Kevin says that those people are "lucky." Kevin says that those people "sold out." Kevin says that those people had connections, advantages, timing, resources that Kevin does not have. Kevin says that those people are not real artists because real artists do not care about publication, real artists create for the sake of creation, real artists are above the crude commerce of selling their work to strangers.

**Kevin is lying.**

Kevin cares enormously about publication. Kevin fantasizes about publication constantly. Kevin imagines the book launch, the interviews, the reviews, the moment when everyone who doubted Kevin is forced to admit they were wrong. Kevin wants all of it. Kevin just does not want to do the thing that makes it possible.

Kevin wants the destination without the journey. Kevin wants the verdict without the exposure. Kevin wants to be called a writer without writing.

So Kevin Declares. And Declares. And Declares again.

And the years pass, and the first chapters accumulate, and the finished manuscripts do not, and Kevin grows older and more defensive and more certain that the problem is external, that the system is rigged, that the gatekeepers are corrupt, that the market is broken, that everyone else is the reason Kevin has not succeeded.

Kevin never asks the question that would end the performance.

Kevin never asks: **What if I am the reason?**

*What if the book is not coming along because I have not written it? What if the agents are not responding because I have not queried them? What if the sales are not happening because there is nothing to sell? What if the silence is not conspiracy but consequence? What if the world is not blocking me from success but simply waiting for me to produce something worth noticing?*

What if the Declaration is the problem?

What if claiming the identity before earning it was the first wrong turn, and every turn since has been an attempt to avoid admitting it? What if the costume has become more important than the work, and the work has withered because the costume fits so well?

**What if I am Kevin?**

That question is unbearable. That question collapses the whole structure. That question forces a choice: either do the work and risk the verdict, or admit that the work was never the point and stop pretending otherwise.

Kevin does not ask that question.

Kevin asks a different question instead. Kevin asks: *Why does no one understand me? Why does no one support me? Why is the world so unfair to people like me?*

Kevin asks those questions loudly, publicly, repeatedly, until the questions become their own answer. Until the asking is the identity. Until Kevin is no longer a writer who has not written but a misunderstood artist whose very lack of output is proof of authenticity.

This is the final form of the Declaration.

This is the Declaration perfected, purified, stripped of any remaining connection to the act it was supposed to describe. This is the Declaration as lifestyle, as brand, as permanent state of becoming that never has to arrive.

This is Kevin. And Kevin is everywhere.

Kevin is in your writing group. Kevin is in your workshop. Kevin is in your online community, your conference, your open mic. Kevin is on your social media feed, posting about the struggle, gathering likes from other Kevins, building a coalition of the incomplete.

**Kevin might be in your mirror.**

If the description fits, do not argue with it. Do not explain why your situation is different. Do not list the legitimate obstacles you have faced, the real challenges you have overcome, the valid reasons you have not yet finished.

The reasons do not matter.

The only thing that matters is the artifact. The only thing that matters is the object that can be held by strangers and judged without mercy. The only thing that matters is the work.

Do the work, or do not.

But stop Declaring.

**The Declaration is a loan against future labor.**

The Declaration is borrowed confidence spent before it is earned. The Declaration is a debt that compounds daily, and the interest rate is your own credibility.

Every time you say "I'm writing a book" without having written one, you deposit a small amount of poison into your own well. Every time you claim the identity without producing the evidence, you make it slightly easier to claim and slightly harder to produce.

The Declaration becomes a habit.

The habit becomes a substitute.

The substitute becomes a prison.

You cannot Declare your way to a finished manuscript. You cannot announce your way to a published book. You cannot identify your way past the lion.

The lion does not care what you call yourself. The lion cares what you put in its mouth. The lion is waiting to see if you have made something that holds.

Have you?

If not, close your mouth. Open the file. Write the next sentence. And do not tell anyone about it until there is something to tell.


*Identity does not precede evidence.*
*If you must say it, you are not it.*

# CHAPTER THREE
## MOTHER BIAS

**Love is blind. The market is 20/20.**

YOUR MOTHER THINKS your book is wonderful.

**Your mother is wrong.**

This is not cruelty.

This is physics.

Your mother loves you. Your mother loved you before you could hold a pencil. Your mother will love you after the book fails, after the dream dies, after you abandon writing entirely and take up woodworking or accounting or quiet desperation.

Her love is unconditional. Her love is absolute. Her love

is the most beautiful and useless thing in the world when it comes to evaluating whether your prose can hold a stranger.

Her feedback is worthless.

This is **Mother Bias**.

Mother Bias is not limited to mothers. It includes fathers, siblings, spouses, partners, childhood friends, college room-mates, and anyone else whose emotional investment in your happiness predates their exposure to your work.

It includes the coworker who wants to be supportive, the neighbor who thinks it is "so cool" that you are writing a book, the online friend who leaves heart emojis on every update. It includes everyone who has a reason to want you to succeed that exists independent of whether you deserve to.

These people are not your readers.

These people are your insulation.

Insulation is warm.

Insulation is comfortable.

Insulation protects you from the cold reality outside.

Insulation is also the thing that will kill you if you mistake it for data.

When your mother reads your manuscript and says "I loved it," she is not lying. She did love it. She loved it because *you* wrote it. She loved it because holding those pages meant holding proof that her child is creative, is special, is doing something meaningful with their life. She loved the artifact not for what it was but for what it represented: you, trying. You, reaching. You, being the person she always believed you could be.

That love is real. That love matters. That love is also completely irrelevant to whether the book works.

A book works when it holds a stranger.

A stranger is someone with no investment in your

success. A stranger is someone who picked up your book because the cover caught their eye or the description intrigued them or they had nothing else to read on the plane. A stranger does not know you. A stranger does not care about your journey. A stranger does not factor in how hard you worked, how much you sacrificed, how long you have been dreaming of this moment.

A stranger reads the first paragraph. A stranger decides, in seconds, whether to read the second. A stranger closes the book and never thinks about it again, or a stranger keeps reading because something in the prose grabbed them and would not let go.

That is the only verdict that matters.

Your mother cannot deliver that verdict. Your mother is constitutionally incapable of delivering that verdict. Asking your mother to evaluate your manuscript is like asking your lungs to evaluate whether you can breathe underwater. The organ is not designed for that function. The organ will tell you what you want to hear because telling you what you want to hear is what the organ does.

Kevin does not understand this.

Kevin shows the manuscript to his mother first. Kevin shows the manuscript to his girlfriend, his best friend, his writing group full of other Kevins who are also showing their manuscripts to each other. Kevin gathers feedback from people who have every reason to be kind and no reason to be honest.

The feedback is glowing. The feedback is always glowing.

*"This is so good." "You really have something here." "I couldn't put it down." "I can't wait to read more." "You should definitely publish this."*

Kevin hears these words and believes them. Why wouldn't Kevin believe them? Multiple people have confirmed the same thing. The consensus is clear. The book is good.

Then Kevin queries an agent.

The agent does not respond.

Kevin queries another agent.

Silence.

Another.

Silence.

Kevin queries thirty agents over six months and receives four form rejections and twenty-six voids of perfect nothingness.

Kevin is confused.

Everyone said the book was good. Everyone said it should be published. Everyone said they loved it. How can the professionals be so wrong? How can the gatekeepers be so blind? How can the industry be so broken that it cannot recognize what Kevin's mother recognized instantly?

Kevin does not consider the alternative explanation.

Kevin does not consider that his mother was not evaluating the book. Kevin does not consider that the consensus was manufactured by selection bias. Kevin does not consider that he has been swimming in warm water so long that he has mistaken temperature for truth.

**Kevin blames the agents.**

This is the trap.

Mother Bias does not just distort the feedback. Mother Bias distorts the interpretation of all feedback that comes after. Once you have been told the work is good by people who love you, you have a baseline. That baseline is wrong, but it feels real, and when reality contradicts it, reality must be the problem.

The agents are wrong. The publishers are wrong. The market is wrong. The readers who did not buy are wrong. Everyone is wrong except the people who told Kevin what he wanted to hear.

This is how insulation becomes armor. This is how the people who love you become the walls of your prison.

They did not mean to imprison you. They meant to support you. They meant to encourage you. They meant to give you the confidence to keep going when the work was hard and the doubt was loud. Their intentions were pure. Their execution was catastrophic.

Because confidence not calibrated to reality is delusion. Because encouragement that ignores evidence is sabotage. Because love that protects you from the truth is the cruelest love of all.

Your mother cannot tell you that your prose is flabby, your pacing is broken, your characters are thin, and your dialogue sounds like an alien's first attempt at human conversation. She cannot tell you this because telling you this would hurt you, and hurting you is something she has been biologically programmed to avoid since before you were born.

Her nervous system will not let her form the words. Her love rewrites the manuscript in real time, smoothing the rough edges, filling the plot holes, translating your clumsy sentences into the book you meant to write.

She reads what she wants to read. She tells you what she read. You believe her.

And the gap between what you wrote and what you think you wrote grows wider with every reassurance.

This is the damage.

The damage is not that you feel good about bad work. The damage is that you lose the ability to see the work clearly. The damage is that the insulation becomes your eyes. The damage is that you cannot tell the difference between prose that holds and prose that is held together by the good-will of people who already decided to love it before they read a word.

The writer who relies on Mother Bias is flying blind.

The writer who relies on Mother Bias has outsourced their quality control to people who are structurally incapable of providing it. The writer who relies on Mother Bias will revise based on feedback that has no relationship to the actual problems in the manuscript, will double down on weaknesses because no one mentioned them, will polish the surface while the foundation rots.

The writer who relies on Mother Bias will never understand why the book failed.

The book will fail.

Not because the market is broken. Not because the agents are blind. Not because readers have no taste. The book will fail because it was never good enough, and no one who loved the writer was willing to say so.

This is not their fault.

This is yours.

You asked the wrong people. You sought comfort when you needed diagnosis. You wanted to hear that you were talented when you needed to hear that page fifty-seven does not work. You built a cocoon of reassurance and called it a support system.

A support system that cannot tell you hard truths is not a support system.

**It is a hospice.**

It is a place where dreams go to be comfortable while they die.

The way out is brutal.

The way out is to stop asking people who love you what they think. The way out is to seek feedback from strangers, from professionals, from people who have no investment in your happiness and every reason to be honest. The way out is to pay for a developmental edit, to join a critique group that includes people who have actually published, to submit to contests where the judges do not know your name.

The way out is to court rejection.

Rejection from strangers is data. Rejection from strangers tells you something real about the gap between what you made and what the market wants. Rejection from strangers hurts precisely because it is not cushioned by love, and that pain is the pain of contact with reality.

Mother Bias protects you from that pain.

Mother Bias keeps you comfortable, keeps you confident, keeps you producing work that will never survive outside the warm circle of people who have already decided to approve.

Kevin lives inside that circle.

Kevin has arranged his entire creative life to avoid leaving that circle. Kevin shows his work only to people who will praise it. Kevin interprets silence from strangers as proof of conspiracy rather than proof of irrelevance. Kevin has built a fortress of affirmation and called it a writing career.

The fortress has no door.

The fortress was not designed to let anything out.

The fortress was designed to keep reality from getting in. And reality, patient as a lion, waits outside.

Your mother cannot save you from the lion.

Your mother cannot query agents for you. Your mother cannot convince publishers to take a chance. Your mother cannot make strangers buy your book or read past the first page or recommend it to their friends. Your mother's love is vast and powerful and absolutely worthless in the marketplace of attention.

**The marketplace does not care who loves you.**

The marketplace cares whether your opening hooks. Whether your middle sustains. Whether your ending satisfies. The marketplace cares whether a person with no reason to care about you will care about your sentences enough to keep reading.

That is the test. That is the only test.

And you cannot prepare for that test by practicing in front of people who have already decided to pass you.

So thank your mother. Mean it. Her love is real, and real love is rare, and you are lucky to have someone who believes in you without requiring proof.

Then close the door. Find someone who does not love you. Show them the work. Listen to what they say without defending, without explaining, without translating their critique into something more comfortable.

If they say it is good, you have data. If they say it needs work, you have better data. If they say nothing and never mention it again, you have the most valuable data of all.

The silence of strangers is the verdict your mother could never give you.

Learn to hear it.

Learn to need it.

Learn to seek it before you seek the warmth.

Because the warmth will always be there. Your mother

will always love your book. Your friends will always say supportive things. The insulation will always be available, always welcoming, always ready to tell you that you are enough exactly as you are.

The insulation is a trap.

Walk into the cold.

Find out what survives.


***If your biggest fan is biologically obligated to love you, you don't have feedback.***

***You have insulation.***

# CHAPTER FOUR
## THE SOMEDAY COLLECTIVE

**If everyone in the room is "working on it,"
no one is working.**

SOMEDAY.

The word sits in the mouth like a mint, sweet and dissolving slowly, leaving nothing behind but the memory of intention. Someday is the most dangerous word in the English language for anyone who has ever wanted to make something.

Someday is where dreams go to hide from deadlines.

Someday is the unmarked grave of ten million unfinished manuscripts.

*Someday I will finish the book.*

*Someday I will query agents.*

*Someday I will self-publish.*

*Someday I will sit down and really focus, really commit, really do the work I have been meaning to do since I first announced that I was doing it.*

**Someday.**

Not today. Today is busy. Today has obligations. Today has a job and a family and errands and exhaustion and a Netflix queue that is not going to watch itself. Today is not the day for the book. Today is the day for everything *except* the book, and tomorrow will be the same, and the day after, and the week after, and the month after, until someday arrives.

Someday never arrives.

Someday is not a day. Someday is a deferral mechanism dressed as a promise. Someday is the lie you tell yourself to avoid the confrontation between what you say you want and what you are actually willing to do to get it.

Kevin lives in Someday.

Kevin has been living in Someday for years. Kevin's entire writing career exists in Someday, a shimmering future state where the book is finished, the agent is interested, the publisher is enthusiastic, the readers are devoted, and all of Kevin's sacrifices have been vindicated.

Someday-Kevin is successful. Someday-Kevin is respected. Someday-Kevin has proven everyone wrong.

**Today-Kevin has written six pages this month.**

The gap between Today-Kevin and Someday-Kevin is not measured in time. It is measured in work. Specifically, it is measured in work that Today-Kevin is not doing.

Every day that passes without production, the gap widens. Every week that ends without pages, Someday recedes further into the fog. Every month that closes with nothing to show, the lie gets harder to maintain.

So Kevin stops measuring.

Kevin stops counting pages. Kevin stops tracking progress. Kevin stops looking at the gap because the gap has become unbearable, and the only way to live with the unbearable is to stop seeing it.

Kevin joins a writing group instead.

The writing group meets weekly. The writing group has other people in it who are also working on books. The writing group provides accountability, community, support. The writing group is a place where Kevin can talk about writing without having to write.

**This is the Someday Collective**.

The Someday Collective is any group of people who have gathered around the shared project of not finishing. They do not describe themselves this way. They describe themselves as writers, as creatives, as artists supporting other artists.

They share goals and deadlines and encouragement. They celebrate small victories: a paragraph completed, a chapter outlined, a character name decided. They treat every forward motion, no matter how microscopic, as proof of progress.

But progress toward what?

Count the finished books in the room. Count the manuscripts that have been completed, revised, polished, and submitted to the judgment of strangers. Count the artifacts that exist independent of the people who made them.

The number is usually zero.

The number is zero because finishing is not the point. The point is the process. The point is the journey. The point is the identity of being someone who is working on something, and that identity does not require completion.

Completion would actually threaten the identity, because completion ends the journey, and ending the journey means facing the verdict.

The Someday Collective exists to prevent the verdict.

The Someday Collective provides an endless supply of acceptable reasons not to finish.

The outline needs more work.

The first act is not quite right.

The research is incomplete.

The voice has not fully emerged.

The story needs to marinate.

The revision needs another pass.

The beta readers have not responded.

The market is not ready.

The timing is not right.

Kevin did not appear because people got worse. Kevin appeared because the environment stopped correcting.

Permission collapsed before judgment adapted. Production became cheap before evaluation became portable. Expression was mistaken for achievement. Access was mistaken for aptitude. Visibility was mistaken for value.

The tools that let anyone publish did not come with tools that let anyone be honest. So declaration replaced evidence. Announcement replaced artifact. And the feedback that once killed bad projects early, silence, rejection, indifference, was reframed as oppression, as gatekeeping, and as cruelty.

Most importantly, isolation ended.

The writer who would once have failed privately now finds others. They form groups. They stabilize each other. They share drafts that never finish. They praise intentions. They narrate process. They call it community.

It is insulation. And in that insulation, Kevin thrives. Not because Kevin is evil. Because Kevin is no longer alone with the silence.

**The silence was the teacher.**
**The teacher has been fired.**

There is always a reason. The reason is always reasonable. And the book is never done.

This is the function of the Collective. Not to help its members finish, but to help them feel okay about not finishing. The Collective normalizes perpetual incompletion. The Collective treats Someday as a legitimate address rather than an evasion. The Collective transforms procrastination into process and avoidance into art.

The members of the Collective tell each other the same stories.

*"Writing is not a race."* True, but irrelevant. It is not a race, but it is also not a state of being. Writing is an act that produces an object. Without the object, the act did not happen. You cannot be a writer without writing, and you cannot claim to be writing if years pass without a finished draft.

*"Everyone works at their own pace."* True, but weaponized. Yes, everyone works at their own pace. Some paces produce books. Some paces produce excuses. The Collective treats all paces as equal, which is a form of kindness that functions as cruelty. A pace of zero words per year is not a pace.

It is a stop.

*"The process is what matters."* False. The process matters only insofar as it produces the artifact. A process that produces nothing is not a process. It is a ritual. It is a performance of work that contains no work. It is the appearance of motion in the absence of movement.

The Collective loves process.

The Collective has extensive conversations about process. Outlining versus pantsing. Morning pages versus evening sessions. Scrivener versus Word versus longhand in Moleskine notebooks. The Collective debates these questions with the intensity of Talmudic scholars, as though the answers matter, as though the right combination of tools and habits will unlock the door that has been closed all along.

The door is not locked.

The door is open. The door has always been open. The only thing required to walk through it is to sit down and write sentences until there are enough sentences to make a book. That is it. That is the entire secret. There is no hack, no method, no optimization that substitutes for the brute accumulation of words in sequence.

The Collective knows this.

The Collective knows this and cannot face it, because facing it would mean admitting that the obstacle is not external. The obstacle is not the process, the pace, the tools, the market, the gatekeepers, or the culture.

The obstacle is the unwillingness to do the work. The obstacle is the preference for Someday over Today. The obstacle is the terror of completion.

Completion is terrifying because completion is exposure.

An unfinished book cannot be rejected. An unfinished book exists in potential, and potential is infinite. An unfinished book could be brilliant. An unfinished book could change the world. An unfinished book is **Schrödinger's Manuscript**, simultaneously a masterpiece and a failure until someone opens the box and collapses the wave function.

Kevin does not want the wave function to collapse.

Kevin wants to live in superposition forever, wants to be both a writer and someone who has not written, wants the identity without the artifact, the credit without the risk. Kevin has found in the Someday Collective a group of people who share this desire, who validate this desire, who have constructed an entire social reality in which this desire is not cowardice but wisdom.

*"There's no rush." "Quality takes time." "Better to get it right than to get it done."*

These mantras circulate through the Collective like prayers, repeated until they become true, or at least true enough to silence the voice that whispers: *you are hiding.*

You are hiding. You have been hiding for years.

You have constructed an elaborate architecture of delay, a cathedral of Someday with stained glass windows depicting all the books you will write when the time is right. You have furnished this cathedral with writing groups and accountability partners and productivity systems and vision boards. You have populated it with fellow believers who tell you that the cathedral is beautiful, that the cathedral is enough, that the cathedral is the destination.

The cathedral is a tomb. The cathedral is where your book went to die without ever being born.

**Someday is a lie you tell the calendar.**

*(Expletive deleted, insert your own)*

That is the truth the Collective cannot speak.

A dream without a deadline is a fantasy. A goal without a timeline is a hope. An intention without a commitment is a story you tell yourself to feel better about not acting.

Deadlines are not cruelty. Deadlines are clarity. Deadlines are the mechanism by which Someday becomes Today, by which intention becomes action, by which the infinite possibility of the unwritten collapses into the finite reality of the written.

The Collective hates deadlines.

The Collective treats deadlines as arbitrary, as stressful, as incompatible with the organic unfolding of the creative process. The Collective prefers open ended commitments, rolling timelines, flexible expectations. The Collective has learned that rigid deadlines produce uncomfortable emotions when they are missed, so the Collective has eliminated rigid deadlines in favor of gentle aspirations.

The gentle aspirations are never met. The gentle aspirations were never meant to be met. The gentle aspirations are permission slips for inaction disguised as respect for the artistic temperament.

Here is what the Collective will not tell you:

Professional writers have deadlines.

Professional writers have contracts with delivery dates.

Professional writers sit down and write even when they do not feel like it, even when the muse is absent, even when the work is hard and the words are ugly and the process feels like dragging a dead body up a hill.

Professional writers finish books not because they are more talented but because they have made a commitment that exists outside their own head, a commitment to an editor, a publisher, a readership that expects delivery.

The Collective has no such commitment.

The Collective answers only to itself, and the self is infinitely forgiving. The self will accept any excuse. The self will grant any extension. The self will renegotiate any deadline into oblivion because the self does not want to finish any more than Kevin does.

Breaking free of the Collective requires an act of violence.

Not physical violence.

Temporal violence.

The violence of choosing a date and treating it as real.

The violence of saying "I will finish the draft by this day" and meaning it, actually meaning it, defending it against all the reasonable reasons why it might need to slide.

The violence of killing Someday.

**Someday must die for Today to live.**

The fantasy of the future perfect book must be sacrificed so that the actual imperfect book can exist. The endless potential must be collapsed into the specific, flawed, vulnerable artifact that will be judged.

This is terrifying.

This is the only way.

The Collective will not support you in this. The Collective will tell you not to rush. The Collective will remind you that quality takes time. The Collective will offer all the mantras that have kept its members safe and unfinished for years.

Thank the Collective for its concern.

Then leave.

Set a deadline. Make it real. Tell someone who will hold you to it, someone outside the Collective, someone who will not accept excuses, someone who will ask on that date: *"Is it done?"*

And then do the work.

Not the process.

Not the ritual.

Not the performance of productivity.

**The work.**

Words on the page, one after another, until the thing is finished.

Finished badly is better than unfinished beautifully. A completed draft can be revised. An incomplete masterpiece is just notes.

The goal is not perfection.

The goal is existence.

The goal is an artifact that can be held, read, judged.

Someday will fight you.

Someday will tell you that you are not ready, that the draft needs more time, that rushing will ruin everything.

Someday will present itself as wisdom, as patience, as self care.

Someday is a liar.

Someday has been lying to you for years.

Someday stole time you will never get back, years you spent preparing for a moment that never came because Someday made sure it couldn't.

Kill Someday.

Set the deadline.

Finish the draft.

Face the lion.

It is the only way out of the Collective. It is the only way to find out whether you are a writer or just someone who has been performing one in the warm company of fellow performers.

The performance ends when the pages exist.

Make them exist.
Today.

**The Someday Collective has no alumni.**

# CHAPTER FIVE
## TRAUMA POSTURING

**The shield protects the person,
but it suffocates the page.**

LET me tell you about my pain.

Let me tell you how I suffered. Let me tell you about the childhood, the loss, the betrayal, the darkness I have walked through to arrive at this moment. Let me tell you about the wound that made me who I am, the scar that shapes my vision, the damage that gives me something to say.

Let me tell you about my pain so that you will understand why my book matters.

This is the gambit. This is the move that has become so common in writing culture that it now functions as credential, as currency, as a kind of preemptive strike against criticism.

The pain comes first. The pain establishes authority. The pain creates a force field around the work that makes evaluation feel like cruelty.

*How can you critique my prose when you know what I have been through? How can you reject my manuscript when you understand the wound it came from? How can you judge my art when my art is my healing?*

**This is Trauma Posturing.**

Trauma Posturing is the strategic deployment of personal suffering as a substitute for craft. It is the conversion of pain into permission. It is the belief that having felt deeply exempts one from the requirement to write well.

It does not.

Your pain is real. Your pain matters. Your pain may be the reason you started writing in the first place, the engine that drove you to the page, the fuel that kept you going when the work was hard. Your pain is valid.

Your pain does not make your sentences correct. Your pain does not fix your pacing. Your pain does not give your characters depth they do not otherwise possess. Your pain does not obligate strangers to read past page ten.

This is the brutal arithmetic of publishing.

The reader does not know you. The reader does not know your history. The reader picks up your book in a store or clicks on it online and encounters the words as words, not as evidence of survival. The reader will not factor in your childhood when evaluating your dialogue. The reader will not adjust expectations based on what you have overcome.

The reader will simply read. And if the reading does not hold, the reader will stop.

No amount of suffering changes this. No depth of wound grants immunity from the market. The artifact must work on its own terms, must grip and sustain and deliver without requiring the reader to know the author's biography.

Kevin does not believe this.

Kevin believes that pain is proof. Kevin has organized an entire creative identity around the wound, has constructed a narrative in which the writing is meaningful because it comes from trauma, is important because it represents healing, is valuable because it cost so much to produce.

Kevin talks about the pain in query letters. Kevin mentions the pain in author bios. Kevin posts about the pain on social media, building an audience not for the work but for the wound, gathering followers who are drawn to the story of suffering rather than the quality of the prose.

This audience is real. This audience may be large. This audience is not a readership.

A readership wants books that work. A readership wants to be transported, entertained, moved, challenged. A readership does not want to perform emotional labor for the author. A readership does not want to be conscripted into someone else's healing process.

But Kevin's audience wants exactly that.

Kevin's audience is composed of people who respond to pain, who valorize suffering, who believe that difficulty confers meaning. Kevin's audience will buy the book out of solidarity, will leave five star reviews out of compassion, will defend the work against criticism as though criticism were attack.

This audience is insulation.

**This audience is Mother Bias scaled to the internet.**

This audience will tell Kevin that the book is beautiful, is brave, is necessary, and Kevin will believe them because Kevin needs to believe them, because the alternative is unbearable.

The alternative is that the pain was real and the book is still not good enough.

That is the thought Trauma Posturing exists to prevent. If the pain justifies the book, then the book cannot fail. If the wound is sufficient credential, then craft is optional. If suffering equals value, then evaluation is assault.

This logic is everywhere in writing culture.

This logic has colonized workshops, conferences, online communities, publishing discourse itself. The question *"Is this good?"* has been replaced by the question *"Is this brave?"* The evaluation of craft has been subordinated to the validation of experience. The artifact has been absorbed by the identity of the person who made it.

This is how critique becomes cruelty.

Once the work is understood as an extension of the wound, any negative assessment is an attack on the wounded person. To say "this chapter does not work" is to say "your pain does not matter." To say "this needs revision" is to say "your healing is insufficient."

The normal operations of feedback, of editing, of the iterative process by which writing improves, become impossible because every suggestion lands on raw nerve.

Kevin cannot be edited.

Kevin's work arrives pre-defended. Kevin's manuscript comes wrapped in biography, surrounded by context, insulated by suffering. To touch the prose is to touch the person. To cut a paragraph is to cut a scar.

Editors learn to recognize this. Agents learn to recognize this.

The recognition usually comes in the query letter, in the sentence that begins "As a survivor of..." or "Having experienced..." or "This book was born from my journey through..."

These sentences are flags. These sentences signal that the author has confused therapeutic expression with commercial product, has mistaken the value of writing for the self with the value of writing for strangers.

The value of writing for the self is immense.

Writing can heal. Writing can process. Writing can transform unspeakable experience into something that can be witnessed, held, understood. Writing can save lives, including the life of the writer. The act of putting words to wound is one of the most powerful technologies humans have developed for surviving their own histories.

None of this means the writing should be published.

Publication is not therapy.

Publication is a marketplace.

Publication is the act of offering an artifact to strangers in exchange for their attention and, usually, their money. The stranger did not ask to participate in your healing. The stranger picked up a book expecting to receive value, not to provide it.

This is the distinction Trauma Posturing collapses.

Trauma Posturing says: my pain entitles me to your attention. My suffering creates an obligation. My wound is so significant that you must witness it, must honor it, must treat my book as important regardless of whether it functions as a book.

The stranger does not agree.

The stranger has their own pain, their own wounds, their own complex inner life. The stranger reads to escape, to learn, to feel, to be transported. The stranger is not looking for another burden. The stranger is not obligated by your history.

The stranger will judge the sentences as sentences. And the sentences, stripped of biographical context, must stand or fall on their own.

Kevin cannot tolerate this.

Kevin has invested everything in the belief that the pain makes the work meaningful. Kevin has built an identity on the idea that suffering and significance are the same thing. Kevin cannot separate the craft from the wound because the wound is all Kevin has.

This is the trap.

The trap is not that trauma makes writing worse. Some of the greatest literature in history has come from wounds. The trap is that trauma makes evaluation feel impossible. The trap is that pain becomes a shield so effective that improvement becomes inconceivable.

How do you revise a scar? How do you edit a wound? How do you suggest that page fifty needs work when page fifty is where the author bled?

You do it anyway.

You do it because the alternative is lying. You do it because the kindest thing you can do for a writer is tell them the truth about their work. You do it because protecting someone from feedback is not protection. It is abandonment. It is leaving them alone with prose that does not function, convinced that the prose is perfect because no one had the courage to say otherwise.

The writer who cannot hear critique cannot improve.

The writer who has armored themselves with suffering is

frozen in place, unable to revise because revision requires admitting that the current version is insufficient. And if the current version came from pain, insufficiency feels like failure of the pain itself.

The pain did not fail. The pain was real. The pain mattered. The pain may have been necessary. The book still does not work.

Both things can be true. Both things are usually true.

The way out is separation.

The way out is learning to see the artifact as separate from the wound, as a made thing that exists independent of its origin, as an object that can be assessed, revised, improved, or abandoned without any of those actions reflecting on the experience that inspired it.

Your pain is yours. No one can take it. No one can invalidate it. No critique of your prose reduces what you survived.

Your book is not your pain.

Your book is a construction made of words that may or may not hold a stranger. Your book can be flawed even though your experience was real. Your book can need work even though your suffering was genuine. Your book can fail even though your healing was necessary.

The market does not trade in pain. The market trades in attention, and attention is won sentence by sentence, page by page, through craft, through skill, through the hard won ability to make a stranger care about what happens next.

Trauma can fuel that ability.

Trauma cannot replace it.

The wound gives you something to say. Craft gives you the ability to say it in a way that lands.

Without craft, the wound is just a wound. Public, visible, demanding witness, but not providing value. The reader approaches expecting a book and finds instead a person bleeding on the page, asking to be seen.

Being seen is not the same as being read. Being witnessed is not the same as being held.

The book must hold. The pain, however real, cannot do that work. Only the sentences can.

So write from the wound if you must. Draw on the darkness. Let the pain fuel the work. Then revise as though the pain does not exist.

Edit with cold eyes. Cut with clean hands. Treat the manuscript as a machine that either functions or does not, and fix the parts that do not function regardless of how much they cost to produce.

This is not betrayal of the experience.

This is respect for it.

The experience deserves a book that works.

Give it one.


***Trauma can justify writing.***
   ***It cannot justify publishing.***

# CHAPTER SIX
## THE FAILURE LADDER

**Gravity is not a conspiracy.**

KEVIN DOES NOT ARRIVE FULLY FORMED.

Kevin is made. Kevin is constructed over time through a series of decisions, each one seemingly reasonable, each one a step further from the verdict that could save him. Kevin is not born. Kevin descends.

There is a ladder, and it only goes down.

The ladder has six rungs. Each rung represents a choice, a threshold crossed, a point at which Kevin traded something real for something that felt like progress but was actually retreat. Each rung is a station on the way to a destination Kevin did not intend to reach but arrived at nonetheless.

The ladder has no reverse.

This is the part Kevin cannot accept. Kevin believes that each decision is temporary, each step can be undone, each threshold can be recrossed in the other direction. Kevin is wrong.

The ladder is structurally one way. Gravity only goes down. The only escape is not climbing back up but jumping off entirely, and jumping off requires producing an artifact that holds.

Until then, Kevin descends.


## RUNG 1: DREAM KEVIN

This is where it begins.

Dream Kevin has an idea for a book. Dream Kevin talks about the idea. Dream Kevin tells friends, family, coworkers, strangers at parties. Dream Kevin has announced the project, has claimed the identity, has begun introducing himself as someone who is "working on something."

Dream Kevin has not written the book.

Dream Kevin may have written notes. Dream Kevin may have an outline, a character sketch, a playlist that captures the vibe. Dream Kevin may have purchased software, attended a workshop, read a book about writing books. Dream Kevin has done everything except the thing that matters.

Dream Kevin is easy to recognize. Dream Kevin speaks in future tense. *"I'm going to write a novel about..." "My book is going to explore..." "When I finish my manuscript, I'm going to..."*

*Going to. Going to. Going to.*

Never done. Never finished. Never here.

Dream Kevin is the most common and most salvageable form. Dream Kevin has not yet invested enough to make retreat painful. Dream Kevin can still wake up, can still recognize that talking about writing is not writing, can still sit down and do the work that transforms announcement into artifact.

Most Dream Kevins do not wake up.

Most Dream Kevins stay at the party, stay in the conversation, stay in the warm space where the book exists as potential and therefore cannot disappoint.

Most Dream Kevins live in Someday until Someday becomes Never, and Never is where they stay.

But some Dream Kevins want more.

Some Dream Kevins grow frustrated with the gap between what they are saying and what they have done. Some Dream Kevins feel the itch of inauthenticity, the sense that the identity is hollow, the knowledge that they cannot keep claiming to be a writer without writing.

These Kevins look for a shortcut. These Kevins descend.

**Transition Trigger:** The first manuscript discussed without pages existing. The moment Kevin speaks about the book as though it is real before making it real. The moment intention becomes identity.


## RUNG 2: HYBRID KEVIN

Hybrid Kevin has decided to take action. Hybrid Kevin is tired of just talking. Hybrid Kevin wants something tangible, something that proves the project is real, something that makes the dream feel closer.

Hybrid Kevin spends money.

Not on craft. Not on editing. Not on the development

that would make the book better. Hybrid Kevin spends money on the appearance of progress. A cover design for a book that does not exist. A website announcing a release date that will never arrive. Business cards that say "Author" above a name that has authored nothing.

Hybrid Kevin discovers the world of services designed to help writers feel like writers without requiring them to write. Logo designers, brand consultants, social media managers, virtual assistants who will manage the platform for the book that has not been written.

Hybrid Kevin invests in infrastructure for an artifact that does not exist.

This feels like progress. This is retreat.

Every dollar spent on appearance is a dollar not spent on substance. Every hour devoted to branding is an hour not devoted to drafting. Hybrid Kevin is building a house of cards and calling it a foundation, constructing an elaborate facade and mistaking it for a building.

But the spending creates commitment.

The spending creates sunk cost. Hybrid Kevin has now invested money, which means Hybrid Kevin must continue or admit the investment was wasted. The spending creates an audience, however small, who expects the book to arrive. The spending creates obligations that did not exist before.

Hybrid Kevin is now trapped by his own initiative.

The book must come. Something must be produced to justify the expenditure, to fulfill the promises, to make the business cards true. But the book still does not exist, and writing it is still hard, and the shortcuts that felt so productive have not made the work any easier.

Hybrid Kevin looks for another shortcut.

**Transition Trigger:** Money spent before readers

exist. The moment Kevin invests in the packaging before creating the product. The moment appearance becomes more real than artifact.

## RUNG 3: VANITY KEVIN

Vanity Kevin has a manuscript.

Vanity Kevin sat down, eventually, and produced pages. The pages may not be good. The pages may not be finished. The pages may be a rough draft that has never seen revision. But the pages exist, and Vanity Kevin is tired of waiting.

Vanity Kevin wants to be published.

Vanity Kevin has tried the traditional route, or claims to have tried it. The agents did not respond. The small presses said no. The system, as far as Vanity Kevin can tell, is broken, biased, impenetrable to outsiders.

Vanity Kevin discovers vanity publishing.

Vanity publishing is the industry that exists to take money from writers in exchange for the appearance of publication. Vanity publishers will print your book. Vanity publishers will give you an ISBN. Vanity publishers will list your book on Amazon, put it in their catalog, send you copies with your name on the spine.

Vanity publishers will not sell your book.

Vanity publishers do not have distribution networks, sales teams, marketing budgets, or relationships with bookstores. Vanity publishers make their money from authors, not from readers. The author is the customer. The book is the product the author buys.

Vanity Kevin does not understand this.

Vanity Kevin sees the listing on Amazon and believes publication has occurred. Vanity Kevin holds the printed book and feels the weight of achievement. Vanity Kevin sends copies to family, posts about the launch, updates the social media bio to say "Published Author."

The book does not sell.

The book does not sell because no one knows it exists.

The book does not sell because it is not in bookstores.

The book does not sell because the cover looks wrong, the interior is poorly formatted, the price is too high, the writing is not ready.

The book does not sell because vanity publishing is designed to extract money from writers, not to deliver books to readers.

Vanity Kevin blames the market.

Vanity Kevin blames Amazon, readers, the death of literacy, the unfairness of the system. Vanity Kevin has done everything right, has invested thousands of dollars, has produced an actual book with an actual cover and actual pages.

How can the world not respond?

The world did respond.

The world responded with silence.

Silence is the verdict. The verdict has been delivered. But Vanity Kevin cannot accept the verdict because the verdict invalidates the investment, the identity, the entire narrative of what was supposed to happen.

Vanity Kevin needs someone else to blame.

**Transition Trigger:** Shortcut replaces audience. The moment Kevin pays for publication instead of earning it. The moment the credential becomes more important than the readership.

. . .

# RUNG 4: CONTRACT KEVIN

Contract Kevin has been approached.

Contract Kevin, still stinging from the vanity experience or still seeking the validation that vanity did not provide, has received an offer. A "publisher" has expressed interest. A "producer" wants to discuss adaptation. An "agent" is excited about the project.

Contract Kevin does not read the contract.

Contract Kevin is too excited, too relieved, too desperate to have the dream validated by an external party. Contract Kevin signs. Contract Kevin celebrates. Contract Kevin announces the deal.

The deal is not what Contract Kevin thinks.

The "publisher" is a hybrid press that requires author investment. The "producer" is a content mill that acquires rights it will never develop. The "agent" is a fee charging operation that makes money from hope, not from sales.

Contract Kevin has signed away rights.

Contract Kevin may have signed away all rights, forever, for all formats, in all territories. Contract Kevin may have agreed to terms that prevent selling the book elsewhere, prevent adapting it independently, prevent walking away even when it becomes clear that nothing is happening.

Contract Kevin did not read the contract. Contract Kevin did not have a lawyer review the contract. Contract Kevin was so hungry for the yes that the terms of the yes did not matter.

Years pass.

The book does not sell. The adaptation does not happen. The "publisher" does not return emails. The rights are locked in a contract that Contract Kevin cannot escape without legal action Contract Kevin cannot afford.

Contract Kevin has lost control of the work.

**Transition Trigger:** Rights clause missed. The moment Kevin trades ownership for validation. The moment the desperation for a yes overwhelms the wisdom to understand what the yes contains.


## RUNG 5: REVERSION KEVIN

Reversion Kevin wants out.

Reversion Kevin has realized, finally, that the contract was a mistake. Reversion Kevin has read the terms, consulted a lawyer, discovered the reversion clause. Reversion Kevin knows that after a certain period of inactivity, or under certain conditions, the rights should return.

Reversion Kevin asks for the rights back. The publisher says no.

The publisher has reasons. The publisher claims the book is still "in print" because a print on demand listing exists. The publisher claims the contract has no reversion clause, or that the conditions for reversion have not been met. The publisher does not respond to emails.

Reversion Kevin is stuck.

Reversion Kevin cannot publish the book elsewhere because someone else owns it. Reversion Kevin cannot adapt the book because someone else controls those rights. Reversion Kevin cannot move forward because the past has been signed away.

Reversion Kevin starts to blame.

Reversion Kevin blames the publisher for being predatory. Reversion Kevin blames the industry for allowing predatory contracts. Reversion Kevin blames the lack of education, the lack of resources, the lack of support for new writers navigating a complex system.

Reversion Kevin does not blame Kevin.

Reversion Kevin does not blame the desperation that led to signing without reading. Reversion Kevin does not blame the hunger for validation that made any yes seem like the right yes. Reversion Kevin does not blame the shortcuts that led, rung by rung, to this place.

Reversion Kevin needs a villain.

**Transition Trigger:** Blame goes public. The moment Kevin begins telling the story of being wronged. The moment the narrative shifts from "I made a mistake" to "I was victimized."


## RUNG 6: THEFT KEVIN

Theft Kevin has found the villain.

Theft Kevin knows who is responsible for everything that went wrong. Theft Kevin has a story, and the story is about theft. Someone stole the dream. Someone stole the rights. Someone stole the success that should have been.

Theft Kevin posts about it.

Theft Kevin warns other writers. Theft Kevin names names. Theft Kevin builds a narrative of persecution in which Kevin is the innocent victim and the world is full of predators, gatekeepers, thieves.

*"Isn't this theft?"* Theft Kevin asks.

The answer is complicated. The contracts may have been predatory, but they were signed. The terms may have been unfair, but they were agreed to. The outcomes may be unjust, but they are legal. The line between "I was deceived" and "I did not read what I signed" is blurry, and Theft Kevin has no interest in clarifying it.

Theft Kevin has reached the bottom of the ladder.

Theft Kevin is no longer a writer. Theft Kevin is a cautionary tale. Theft Kevin spends more energy warning others than producing new work, more time litigating the past than building the future.

Theft Kevin will never write another book.

Not because the industry stole the ability. Because the grievance has become the identity. Because being wronged has replaced being productive. Because the story of what happened to Kevin has become more important than any story Kevin might write.

This is the final form. This is where the ladder ends.


## THE EXIT

The ladder has no reverse.

You cannot climb back up. You cannot undo the decisions, reclaim the rights you signed away, un-spend the money, un-tell the lies you told yourself. The ladder is a record of choices, and choices have consequences that compound.

But you can jump.

You can jump by producing an artifact that holds.

Not talking about it. Not paying someone to package it. Not signing it away to anyone who shows interest. Producing it. Finishing it. Revising it until it works. Submitting it to judgment that is real, to readers who are strangers, to a market that does not care about your history on the ladder.

The artifact that holds erases the ladder.

The artifact that holds proves that everything before was

prelude, not destiny. The artifact that holds demonstrates that Kevin was a phase, not a permanent condition. The artifact that holds is the only exit.

Everything else is further descent.

If you recognize yourself on this ladder, stop.

Stop where you are.

Do not take the next step.

Do not look for the shortcut that will solve the problem the last shortcut created.

Do not spend, sign, or speak.

Sit down. Write the book. Make it work.

The ladder only goes down.

But you do not have to keep climbing.


**The ladder has no reverse.**
   **Only escape through output.**

# CHAPTER SEVEN
## TALENT IS NOT EVENLY DISTRIBUTED

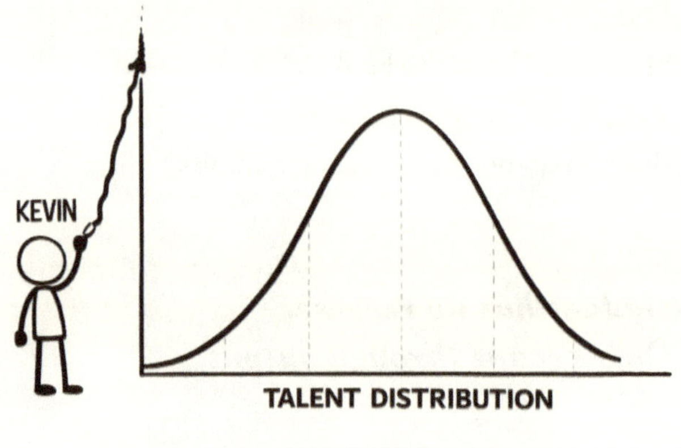


**You can edit the manuscript.**
**You cannot edit the curve.**

HERE IS a truth so obvious it should not need saying, and so inflammatory it cannot be said:

**Some people are better than other people at things.**

Some people run faster. Some people see farther. Some people hear pitch with precision that others will never achieve regardless of practice. Some people possess, from birth or early development, capacities that others do not possess and cannot acquire.

This is true of writing.

Some people have an ear for sentences. Some people do not. Some people can feel the weight of a word, the rhythm of a paragraph, the architecture of a scene. Some people read their own prose and know, without being told, where it sags. Some people cannot hear what they have written no matter how many times they read it aloud.

This is not fair. This is not a moral judgment. This is not a statement about human worth, dignity, or the right to pursue happiness. This is just true.

Kevin cannot tolerate this truth.

Kevin has built an entire worldview on its opposite. Kevin believes that talent is evenly distributed, that everyone has a book in them, that the only difference between a published author and an unpublished one is opportunity, persistence, or luck. Kevin believes that desire is proof of capacity, that wanting to write well is the same as being able to write well, that the universe would not have given Kevin this dream if Kevin were not meant to achieve it.

Kevin is wrong.

The universe does not distribute dreams based on capacity. The universe does not ensure that longing aligns with ability. The universe is not a meritocracy, but it is also not a participation trophy factory. The universe simply is, and within it, abilities vary.

This variance is dramatic.

At one end of the distribution, there are people who will never write a readable sentence regardless of how many workshops they attend, how many books on craft they consume, how many hours they put into practice. Their ceiling is low. Their prose will always be functional at best, awkward at worst. They can improve, but improvement has limits, and their limits are lower than others.

At the other end, there are people who write beautifully almost by accident. Their first drafts contain sentences that others labor years to approximate. Their instincts are calibrated. Their ear is tuned. They do not know why their prose works because they have never experienced prose that does not work. For them, writing well is like breathing. They cannot explain it any more than you can explain how you walk.

Most people are in the middle.

Most people have some capacity, some ear, some feel for language. Most people can improve significantly with practice and feedback. Most people, with enough work, can produce prose that is competent, readable, perhaps even good.

**But most people will not produce prose that is exceptional.**

This is arithmetic, not cruelty.

Exceptional is, by definition, the exception. If everyone could achieve it, it would not be exceptional. The bell curve exists. The tails are thin. The middle is crowded. Most writers, no matter how hard they work, will produce work that is average, because average is where most of the distribution lives.

Kevin finds this intolerable.

Kevin has been told, since childhood, that hard work conquers all. Kevin has absorbed the myth that persistence is the only variable, that grit is destiny, that anyone can achieve anything if they just want it badly enough. Kevin has internalized a story about human potential that is motivational poster wisdom mistaken for reality.

**The motivational posters lied.**

Hard work matters. Persistence matters. Grit matters.

But they matter as multipliers applied to a base, and the base varies.

- Hard work **x** High talent **=** Exceptional results.
- Hard work **x** Modest talent **=** Good results.
- Hard work **x** Minimal talent **=** Results that are better than no work but still below the threshold where strangers will pay attention.

This is not pessimism. This is calibration.

The writer who understands their own capacity can make intelligent decisions. The writer who accurately assesses their ceiling can choose appropriate goals. The writer who knows they will never be literary can decide to be commercial, to be entertaining, to be useful in ways that do not require genius.

The writer who insists they have no ceiling will crash into it repeatedly and blame the crash on everything except the ceiling.

Kevin crashes constantly.

Kevin queries agents with manuscripts that are not ready and interprets the silence as conspiracy. Kevin self publishes books that do not sell and blames the algorithm. Kevin enters contests and does not place and concludes that the judges are biased. Kevin does everything except consider the possibility that the work itself is the problem.

The work is usually the problem.

Not because Kevin does not try. Kevin tries hard. Kevin has read the books on craft. Kevin has attended the workshops. Kevin has put in the hours. Kevin has done everything the motivational posters said to do.

The motivational posters did not mention the base.

The motivational posters did not mention that effort is the entry fee, not the guarantee. The motivational posters did not mention that millions of people pay the entry fee and most of them do not win. The motivational posters sold a fantasy of unlimited potential because unlimited potential is an easier sell than the truth.

The truth is harder.

The truth is that you might work your entire life and never produce a book that strangers want to read. The truth is that your ceiling might be lower than your ambition. The truth is that the dream you have carried since childhood might be a dream you are not equipped to achieve.

This does not make you worthless. This does not make your life meaningless. This does not make your effort wasted.

It just means that this particular dream, in this particular form, might not be yours to catch.

Kevin cannot hear this.

Kevin hears this and translates it into an attack on Kevin's personhood. Kevin hears "your writing might not be good enough" and receives "you are not good enough as a human being." Kevin has so thoroughly merged identity with aspiration that any limitation on the aspiration feels like a limitation on the self.

**This is the trap.**

The trap is not that talent varies. The trap is that Kevin has made talent the measure of worth. The trap is that Kevin cannot accept being average at writing because Kevin has decided that being average at writing means being average as a person.

You are not your writing.

Your writing is a thing you do. It is not a thing you are. Your capacity to arrange words in pleasing sequences has no bearing on your value as a friend, a parent, a citizen, a human being. Your inability to write a novel that sells does not diminish your right to exist, to be loved, to find meaning.

But Kevin has forgotten this.

Kevin has staked everything on the writing. Kevin has made the dream the center of identity, has organized an entire life around the assumption that the writing will eventually succeed, has deferred happiness until the verdict arrives.

When the verdict does not arrive, or arrives negative, Kevin has nothing left.

This is why Kevin cannot hear the truth about talent.

The truth is too expensive. The truth would require rebuilding an identity from scratch. The truth would require admitting that years were spent pursuing a goal that was never achievable, that the foundation was sand, that the castle was always going to fall.

So Kevin denies the truth.

Kevin insists that talent is evenly distributed. Kevin insists that the only variable is effort, persistence, luck. Kevin insists that success is a matter of finding the right hack, the right platform, the right moment. Kevin insists that the ceiling does not exist, that the base does not matter, that wanting is the same as being able.

Kevin is building a **Theology of Denial**.

The theology has many believers. The theology is comforting. The theology says that you are special, that your dream is valid, that the universe wants you to succeed. The theology fills conference halls and sells books on craft and populates online communities where everyone agrees that everyone can make it.

The theology is a lie.

Not everyone can make it. Not everyone will produce work that strangers want to read. Not everyone has the capacity, regardless of effort, to cross the threshold from amateur to professional.

This is not injustice. This is the distribution of ability in a species of eight billion.

Someone has to be average. Someone has to be below average. Someone has to be significantly below average while believing they are significantly above.

The question is not whether this is fair. It is not fair. The question is what you do with the knowledge.

You can deny it. You can spend decades insisting that your ceiling does not exist, crashing into it, blaming the crash on external forces. You can join Kevin in the theology of unlimited potential and die mid sentence, still explaining why the world was wrong about you.

Or you can accept it.

You can look clearly at your own work, compare it honestly to work that succeeds, and assess where you actually stand. You can ask whether your ceiling is high enough to achieve your goals, and if it is not, you can adjust the goals. You can decide that being a competent amateur is enough, that writing for yourself and your circle is meaningful, that the dream does not have to scale to the size of the industry to be worth having.

You can be a writer without being a professional. You can create without selling. You can love the craft without demanding that the craft love you back.

This is not giving up. This is growing up.

The child believes that wanting something is enough to get it. The adult learns that wanting is common, capacity varies, and outcomes depend on the intersection of the two.

The adult makes peace with limitation. The adult finds meaning in what is possible rather than raging against what is not.

Kevin never grows up.

Kevin stays in the childhood belief forever, insisting that the ceiling is a lie, that the variance is a conspiracy, that someday the truth will be revealed and Kevin will be vindicated.

Someday does not come.

The ceiling is real.

The variance is real.

Your capacity is what it is.

Work will improve it. Practice will refine it. Feedback will calibrate it. But at some point, you will reach the limit of what work, practice, and feedback can do, and the limit will be wherever it is, not wherever you want it to be.

If the limit is high enough, you will succeed. If the limit is not high enough, you will not.

Both are acceptable outcomes. Neither determines your worth. But only one of them is compatible with reality, and reality is where the readers live.


***Effort is the entry fee.***
   ***The market decides the value.***

# CHAPTER EIGHT
## AUDIENCE SUBSTITUTION

**Likes are free. Books cost time.**

## KEVIN HAS FOLLOWERS.

Kevin has built something that looks like an audience. There are numbers attached to Kevin's name on platforms: followers, subscribers, members of a mailing list, participants in a Discord server. Kevin can point to these numbers as evidence of traction, of relevance, of the market responding to what Kevin has to offer.

Kevin does not have readers.

Kevin has an audience that watches Kevin *be* a writer. This is different from an audience that reads what Kevin *writes*.

The first audience is there for Kevin. The second audience is there for the work. The first audience will like, comment, share, and support. The second audience will buy, read, and recommend.

Kevin has confused the first for the second.

This is **Audience Substitution**.

Audience Substitution is the mistake of treating social engagement as market validation. It is the belief that followers are readers, that likes are sales, that the attention gathered on platforms translates directly to the attention required for a book to succeed.

It does not.

The currencies are different. The economies are separate. The person who follows you on social media because they find your posts entertaining is not the same person who will spend money and hours on your book. The relationship between posting and publishing is not linear. It is barely related.

Kevin does not understand this.

Kevin has spent years building a following. Kevin has posted consistently, engaged authentically, grown the numbers through the approved methods. Kevin has done everything the advice says to do: build a platform, establish a presence, create an audience before you have a product.

Kevin has the platform. Kevin has the presence. Kevin has the audience.

Kevin's book does not sell.

The followers do not convert. The likes do not translate. The engagement that felt so real, so encouraging, so much like proof of demand, evaporates when confronted with the ask: *buy this book and read it.*

Buying is different from following. Reading is different from scrolling.

The attention economy of social media is designed to extract small, frequent, frictionless engagements. A like costs nothing. A follow requires one click. A comment takes seconds. The entire architecture is built to minimize commitment and maximize volume.

Books require the opposite.

Books require a single person to commit money and hours to a single artifact. Books are not snackable. Books are not scrollable. Books demand sustained attention, and sustained attention is the scarcest resource in the modern economy, far scarcer than follows or likes.

Kevin's audience was trained in the wrong currency.

Kevin's audience learned to engage with Kevin in the low commitment patterns that platforms reward. Quick reactions. Brief interactions. The dopamine hit of notification without the investment of attention. When Kevin asks this audience to shift currencies, to convert their low commitment engagement into high commitment reading, most of them decline.

Not because they do not like Kevin. Because liking someone on social media is not the same as wanting to read their book.

The conflation of these two things is one of the great deceptions of modern publishing advice. "Build your platform" has become gospel, repeated so often and so confidently that writers believe it is the path to success. Build the platform and the readers will come. Grow the following and the sales will follow.

The data does not support this.

The writers with the largest social media followings are

not reliably the writers with the best selling books. The correlation between platform size and book sales is weak, noisy, and frequently negative. Some of the most successful books come from writers with minimal online presence. Some of the largest platforms belong to writers whose books disappear without impact.

The platform is not the product. The platform is a distraction that feels like work.

Kevin loves the platform.

Kevin loves the platform because the platform provides immediate feedback. Post something, get likes. Share an update, receive encouragement. The platform is responsive in a way that writing is not. The platform tells Kevin, constantly and instantly, that Kevin matters.

The manuscript provides no such feedback.

The manuscript sits in silence. The manuscript does not like your updates. The manuscript does not validate your existence. The manuscript just waits, demanding work, offering nothing until the work is complete and submitted to judgment that may never arrive.

So Kevin works on the platform instead.

Kevin spends hours crafting posts, responding to comments, growing the following. Kevin tells himself this is work, this is building toward the goal, this is laying the foundation for success. Kevin's time disappears into the platform, and the manuscript remains unfinished.

The platform ate the book.

This is the second function of Audience Substitution. It does not just misrepresent the relationship between following and reading. It actively steals the time and energy that should go to writing. Every hour on the platform is an hour not on the page. Every burst of dopamine from engagement is a burst not earned through creation.

Kevin becomes addicted to the substitute.

Kevin cannot write without checking engagement. Kevin cannot draft without the phone nearby, waiting for the notification that proves Kevin exists. Kevin has outsourced self worth to the platform, and the platform demands constant feeding, and the feeding leaves nothing for the work.

The work starves. The platform thrives. Kevin has thousands of followers and no finished book.

But there is a deeper problem.

The platform does not just steal time. The platform distorts perception. The platform creates an echo chamber in which Kevin's voice is constantly reflected back, amplified, validated.

Kevin posts about writing. Kevin's followers, who are also aspiring writers, agree with what Kevin says. Kevin's followers share Kevin's frustrations about the industry, the gatekeepers, the unfairness. Kevin's followers create a consensus reality in which Kevin's view of the world is the correct view.

This is Audience Substitution in its most dangerous form.

Kevin has replaced the judgment of the market with the judgment of the crowd. Kevin has substituted the verdict of strangers for the approval of followers. Kevin has created a bubble in which Kevin is always right, always talented, always deserving of success that the corrupt system refuses to provide.

The crowd agrees.

The crowd always agrees.

**The crowd is not the market.**

The market is composed of strangers who do not follow Kevin, do not know Kevin, do not care about Kevin. The market is composed of people browsing bookstores, scrolling retailer pages, looking for something to read without any prior relationship to the author. The market does not know Kevin exists. The market will encounter the book, if it encounters the book at all, as an object that must justify its own existence.

Kevin's crowd cannot help with this.

Kevin's crowd is invisible to the market. Kevin's crowd's enthusiasm does not appear on the book's cover. Kevin's crowd's likes do not show up in the sample pages. When the stranger in the bookstore picks up Kevin's book, the stranger knows nothing about the thousands of followers, the years of engagement, the community that believes in Kevin.

The stranger sees only the words. The stranger judges only the words. The stranger decides, based only on the words, whether to continue.

If the words do not hold, the stranger puts the book down and never thinks about Kevin again. The platform, the following, the community, the years of audience building evaporate. They were never relevant. They were a parallel universe that had no bearing on the transaction that mattered.

Kevin's crowd will be sad.

Kevin's crowd will post supportive messages. Kevin's crowd will insist that the market is wrong, that Kevin's book deserved better, that the system is broken. Kevin's crowd will provide the same reassurance it has always provided, the same validation, the same protection from the truth.

The truth is simple.

**Agreement is not authority.**

The crowd agreeing with Kevin does not make Kevin right. The followers validating Kevin does not make Kevin's book good. The platform applauding Kevin does not make the prose hold. Consensus among people who already like you is the easiest consensus to achieve and the least valuable.

Kevin needs disagreement.

Kevin needs readers who have no reason to be kind. Kevin needs strangers who will judge the work on its merits. Kevin needs the market, not the crowd.

But the market is scary.

The market is indifferent. The market does not care about Kevin's feelings. The market will render a verdict that cannot be explained away, that cannot be attributed to bias, that cannot be dismissed as the opinion of people who just do not understand.

The crowd is safe. The crowd is warm. The crowd is where Kevin hides.

The way out is inversion.

The way out is to stop measuring success by engagement and start measuring it by sales, by reads, by recommendations from strangers. The way out is to recognize the platform for what it is: a distraction that feels productive, a substitute that feels real, a crowd that feels like a market but is not.

The way out is to write the book.

Not post about writing the book. Not build an audience for the book you have not written. Not substitute the performance of being a writer for the act of writing.

Write the book. Finish the book. Submit the book to strangers. Let the strangers judge.

The strangers are the market. The strangers are the only verdict that matters.

Your followers will still be there after the verdict. Your crowd will still support you. Your platform will still provide the dopamine you have come to need.

But none of that is the work. The work is the book. The book is the only thing the market can see.

Make it visible.

**Followers are not readers.**
**The crowd is not the market.**

# CHAPTER NINE
## THE MARKET IS NOT RIGGED

**The storm does not know your name.**

## THE MARKET HATES YOU.

This is what Kevin believes.

The market is a conspiracy, a cabal, a rigged game designed to keep people like Kevin out. The market has gatekeepers who guard the gates not based on quality but on connections, credentials, demographics, and luck. The market is a machine built to crush dreams, and Kevin's dream has been crushed, and the machine is to blame.

Kevin is wrong.

The market does not hate Kevin.

**The market does not know Kevin exists.**

This is worse.

Hatred requires attention. Hatred requires the hater to notice the hated, to expend energy on them, to care enough to oppose. The market does none of these things. The market is not a person. The market is not a committee. The market is not a shadowy organization meeting in secret to decide whose books will succeed and whose will fail.

The market is the aggregate behavior of millions of strangers making individual choices about how to spend their attention.

That is all. That is everything.

The market is a reader scrolling past your cover because something else caught their eye. The market is a browser clicking away from your sample page because the first paragraph did not hook. The market is a customer choosing the book next to yours on the shelf because the other book looked more interesting.

The market is silence, accumulated across millions of micro decisions, none of which were about you.

The market is not rigged against you. The market is indifferent to you.

Kevin cannot tolerate indifference.

Indifference is unbearable because indifference removes Kevin from the story. If the market is rigged, Kevin is a victim, and victims are protagonists, and protagonists matter. If the market hates Kevin, Kevin is significant enough to be hated. If there is a conspiracy, Kevin is important enough to be conspired against.

But if the market is simply indifferent, Kevin is nothing.

Kevin is noise in a system that processes millions of signals. Kevin is one of ten thousand query letters an agent receives in a year. Kevin is one of four million books available on the largest retailer.

Kevin is invisible, unnoticed, unremarkable, lost in a sea of other people who also want attention and are also not getting it.

This is the truth Kevin's conspiracy theories are designed to obscure.

The theories are elaborate. The algorithms are suppressing Kevin's book. Amazon is burying it. The retailers are favoring traditional publishers. The agents only want celebrities. The editors only want diverse voices, or only want white voices, or only want whatever Kevin is not. The system is broken in a specific way that explains Kevin's specific failure.

Every theory has evidence.

Every theory can point to examples, anecdotes, articles, posts from other writers who share the same grievance. Every theory creates a community of believers who reinforce each other's belief. Every theory feels true because every theory provides an explanation that is more bearable than the alternative.

The alternative is that the book was not good enough. The alternative is that Kevin's prose did not hold. The alternative is that the market, in its vast indifferent aggregate, encountered Kevin's work and collectively shrugged.

This cannot be.

If Kevin's work is not good enough, then Kevin is not good enough. If the prose did not hold, then the years were wasted. If the market shrugged, then Kevin is ordinary, and Kevin has built an entire identity on being extraordinary.

So the market must be rigged.

The market is not rigged.

The market is chaotic, noisy, unpredictable, and often unfair. Good books fail. Bad books succeed. Lightning strikes randomly. The cream does not always rise. The system contains genuine inefficiencies, biases, and broken feedback loops.

None of this makes it rigged.

Rigged implies intention. Rigged implies a rigger. Rigged implies that someone, somewhere, decided that Kevin specifically would not succeed. This is grandiosity disguised as grievance. The universe does not care enough about Kevin to rig anything against Kevin.

The market is a **Weather System**.

You do not blame the weather for raining on your parade. You do not accuse the clouds of conspiracy. You do not organize support groups for other people whose parades were rained on. You accept that weather is weather, that rain is rain, that sometimes it falls on you and sometimes it does not.

The market is the same.

Sometimes your book finds its readers. Sometimes it does not. Sometimes the timing is right. Sometimes it is wrong. Sometimes the cover works. Sometimes it repels. Sometimes the algorithm surfaces you. Sometimes it buries you. The variables are so numerous, so chaotic, so interdependent that predicting outcomes is nearly impossible.

This is not rigging. This is complexity.

Kevin wants the complexity to be simple. Kevin wants a villain.

Villains are useful. Villains provide a target for anger. Villains explain failure in a way that preserves Kevin's self image. Villains transform "I did not succeed" into "I was prevented from succeeding," and the difference between those two sentences is the difference between responsibility and victimhood.

Kevin chooses victimhood. Kevin blames the algorithms.

The algorithms are real. The algorithms do shape discovery. The algorithms do favor certain content over other content. The algorithms are opaque, unpredictable, and frequently frustrating. But the algorithms are not a conspiracy against Kevin.

The algorithms are optimization engines trying to show people what they are most likely to engage with. The algorithms learn from behavior: what people click, what they buy, what they read, what they finish. The algorithms are mirrors reflecting collective preference back at the collective.

If the algorithms are not showing Kevin's book, it is because the data suggests people are not interested in Kevin's book.

This is not the algorithm's fault. This is feedback.

Kevin refuses to hear it. Kevin blames the gatekeepers.

The gatekeepers are real. Agents reject most queries. Publishers reject most submissions. The traditional path is narrow, and most writers do not fit through it. The gatekeeping function is genuine, and it excludes more than it includes.

But the gatekeepers are not a conspiracy.

The gatekeepers are people doing jobs. Their job is to find books they can sell. Their job is to filter signal from noise in an environment that is almost entirely noise. Their job requires saying no hundreds of times for every yes, and the math of their job means most writers will receive no.

This is not personal.

The agent who did not respond to Kevin did not read Kevin's query and think "*I will destroy this person's dreams.*"

The agent read Kevin's query, or more likely the first paragraph of Kevin's query, determined it was not something they could sell, and moved on. The entire process took seconds.

Kevin was not considered, weighed, and rejected. Kevin was glanced at and passed.

This is worse than rejection. This is irrelevance.

Kevin cannot tolerate irrelevance.

So Kevin builds a theory in which the gatekeepers are corrupt, biased, incompetent, blind to true talent. Kevin finds other writers who share this theory. Kevin constructs a community of the rejected in which rejection is proof of quality, in which the gatekeepers are the enemy, in which not being chosen is a badge of honor.

This community is large. This community is loud. This community changes nothing.

The gatekeepers continue gatekeeping. The algorithms continue optimizing. The market continues being indifferent to millions of books while paying attention to thousands. The system does not notice Kevin's grievance, does not respond to Kevin's accusations, does not adjust itself to accommodate Kevin's dreams.

The system is not a person. The system cannot be shamed into fairness. The system cannot be argued into compliance. The system simply is.

Kevin can spend a lifetime raging against it. Kevin can build an identity around opposition to it. Kevin can gather followers who share the rage and the opposition. Kevin can die having never published successfully, confident to the end that the failure was the system's fault.

Or Kevin can do something else.

Kevin can accept that the market is not rigged. Kevin can

accept that the market is indifferent. Kevin can accept that indifference is not injustice.

Kevin can ask a different question.

Instead of *"Why is the market rigged against me?"* Kevin can ask *"What would make the market notice me?"*

The answer to the first question is always external. The conspiracy, the algorithm, the gatekeepers, the bias. The answer to the first question always points away from Kevin, away from the work, away from anything Kevin can control.

The answer to the second question is internal.

**What would make the market notice?**

Better prose. Sharper hooks. Cleaner structure. A cover that signals genre correctly. A description that promises value. A sample that delivers on the promise. A book that holds a stranger who has no reason to care.

These things are within Kevin's control. These things are the work.

The conspiracy theory is comfortable because it eliminates the work. If the market is rigged, no amount of improvement will help. If the game is fixed, playing better is pointless. The conspiracy theory grants permission to stop trying, to stop improving, to stop doing the hard thing and instead do the easy thing, which is complaining.

Complaining is easy. Complaining gathers agreement. Complaining builds community. Complaining produces nothing that the market can see.

The market sees only books. The market judges only books. The market does not care about your theory of why the market should have treated you differently.

The market asks one question: **Does this hold me?**

If yes, the market pays attention. If no, the market moves on.

That is all the market does. It is not rigged. It is not corrupt. It is not conspiring.

It is just vast, and you are small, and the vast thing does not notice the small thing unless the small thing produces something remarkable enough to be noticed.

Produce something remarkable. That is the only answer. That has always been the only answer.

The conspiracy theory is a detour. The grievance is a trap. The community of the rejected is a hospice for dreams that refused to get better.

Get better. Make the work better. Submit the better work to the indifferent market. See what happens.

If it fails, make it better again. Repeat until the market notices or until you decide that the market's attention is not worth the effort required to earn it.

Both are acceptable outcomes. Neither requires believing the game is fixed.

The game is not fixed.

The game is hard.

Play it or don't.

But stop blaming the rules for your score.


***Algorithms may distort exposure.***
  ***They do not distort indifference.***

# CHAPTER TEN
## THE AI EXCUSE

**If a machine can replace your soul,**

**you didn't have one.**

THE ROBOTS ARE COMING for your job.

This is the fear. This is the excuse. This is the newest entry in Kevin's catalog of reasons why the dream is dying and the death is not Kevin's fault.

Artificial intelligence can write now. AI can produce prose, generate stories, draft novels. AI can do in seconds what used to take months. The machines have learned to string words together, and the words are coherent, and the coherence is terrifying to people who believed that stringing words together was their special gift.

Kevin is terrified.

Kevin has watched the demos. Kevin has seen the outputs. Kevin has read the breathless articles about the end of writing as a human endeavor. Kevin has concluded that the game is over, that the machines have won, that there is no point in continuing because the robots will do it better, faster, cheaper.

Kevin is wrong.

Not about the technology. The technology is real. The technology is impressive. The technology will continue to improve. The machines can generate text that passes casual inspection, that reads as competent, that fills space adequately.

Kevin is wrong about what this means.

Kevin believes that writing was about generating text. Kevin believes that the hard part was getting words onto the page, and now that machines can do that, the hard part has been automated away.

Kevin never understood what the hard part was.

The hard part was never generating text.

**The hard part was judgment.**

The hard part was knowing which words to keep and which to cut. The hard part was sensing when a scene was working and when it was dying. The hard part was feeling the rhythm of a paragraph and adjusting it until it sang. The hard part was the ten thousand decisions, conscious and unconscious, that separate prose that holds from prose that fills space.

AI cannot do this.

**AI can generate. AI cannot judge.**

AI produces text the way a fire hose produces water: volume without direction. AI does not know if the sentence it just wrote is good. AI does not know if the paragraph serves the story. AI does not know if the chapter earns its place in the book. AI has no sense of quality because AI has no sense. AI is a pattern matching engine that predicts the next likely token based on statistical distributions in training data.

**This is not writing.**

**This is autocomplete at scale.**

The writer who understands this has nothing to fear from AI. The writer who understands this can use AI as a tool, can generate drafts to react against, can produce raw material to refine. The writer who understands this knows that the value was never in the generation. The value was in the curation, the selection, the shaping of raw material into something that works.

Kevin does not understand this. Kevin thought the magic was in the typing.

Kevin spent years typing, producing pages, generating text. Kevin believed that the pages were the achievement, that the volume was the measure, that finishing the draft was the goal.

The draft was never the goal. The goal was a book that holds.

AI can produce drafts. AI can produce infinite drafts. AI can fill every hard drive on the planet with drafts. None of those drafts will hold a stranger unless a human being with judgment shapes them into something that works.

That human being is still necessary. That human being is still the author.

The author is not the person who typed the words. The author is the person who decided which words to keep.

But Kevin has found a different use for AI. Kevin has found that AI is an excellent excuse.

Kevin can now explain failure in a new way. The market is flooded with AI content. The readers cannot find human work amid the machine generated noise. The algorithms favor volume, and AI produces volume, so human writers are drowned out.

This theory is seductive. This theory contains elements of truth.

The market is noisier. Discovery is harder. Volume has increased. These things are real.

But they do not explain Kevin's failure.

Kevin was failing before AI. Kevin was not selling before the machines started writing. Kevin was being ignored when every word in the market was typed by a human hand. The flood of AI content did not cause Kevin's irrelevance. It merely provided a new explanation for a preexisting condition.

Kevin was drowning before the flood. The water was already over Kevin's head. The AI flood just made it easier to blame the water.

This is the function of the AI excuse. Not to explain what is happening, but to preserve Kevin's self image in the face of what was already happening. The excuse is a life raft that keeps Kevin afloat in the narrative where Kevin is a victim rather than a participant.

Meanwhile, writers who understand judgment are adapting.

Writers who understand judgment are using AI as a tool rather than fearing it as a replacement. Writers who understand judgment are generating drafts with AI and then applying human discernment to make those drafts work. Writers who understand judgment are producing more, experimenting faster, iterating quickly because the cost of generation has dropped to zero.

The cost of judgment has not dropped.

**The cost of judgment has increased.**

When anyone can generate text, the ability to distinguish good text from bad becomes more valuable, not less. When the market is flooded with *competent but soulless prose,* the prose that has soul stands out more, not less. When the machines can produce the average, the above average becomes more precious.

Kevin could benefit from this. Kevin could develop judgment.

Kevin could learn to feel the difference between prose that works and prose that merely exists. Kevin could train the ear that hears when a sentence is alive. Kevin could cultivate the instinct that knows when to cut and when to keep.

Kevin does not do this. Kevin is too busy being afraid.

Kevin is too busy explaining to anyone who will listen that AI has ruined everything. Kevin is too busy gathering with other Kevins to mourn the death of human creativity.

Human creativity is not dead. Human creativity was never about generating text.

Human creativity is about judgment, taste, discernment, the ineffable sense of what works that cannot be reduced to statistical patterns because it emerges from lived human experience.

AI does not have lived human experience.

AI has ingested the text that humans produced from lived experience. AI can mimic the surface patterns of that text. AI cannot generate new meaning because AI does not know what meaning is. AI cannot write from wound because AI has never been wounded. AI cannot capture the specific texture of a human life because AI has not lived one.

This is not mysticism. This is observation.

Read AI prose carefully. Read it not for competence but for presence. Ask whether there is a there there, whether something is being said or whether words are being arranged in patterns that suggest something is being said.

The difference is subtle. The difference is everything.

The prose that holds has presence. The prose that holds contains a mind making choices, a sensibility filtering experience, a human being trying to communicate something true to another human being. This presence cannot be faked because it emerges from the thing AI lacks: a self.

AI has no self. AI has a very sophisticated model of how selves write. The model can produce passable imitations. The imitations do not hold.

Kevin cannot tell the difference. Kevin never could tell the difference.

Kevin's prose was always imitation, not presence. Kevin was always mimicking the surface patterns of good writing without understanding what made the writing good. Kevin was always producing text that looked like the text that worked without knowing why the text that worked worked.

This is why Kevin fears AI.

**Kevin recognizes a competitor.**

Kevin has been doing manually what AI does automatically: producing text that resembles good writing without containing the judgment that makes writing good. Kevin has been a human autocomplete, predicting what a writer would say without having anything to say.

AI does this better. AI does this faster. AI does this cheaper.

Kevin is being outcompeted at Kevin's own game.

But the game Kevin was playing was never the real game.

The real game was not about producing text. The real game was about producing meaning. The real game required judgment, presence, self. The real game was never going to be won by pattern matching, whether the pattern matcher was silicon or carbon.

The writers who understand this are not afraid.

The writers who understand this welcome AI as a tool that handles the parts of writing that were never the point. Generation was never the point. The blank page was never the enemy. The enemy was always the absence of judgment, the inability to tell good from bad, the lack of discernment that left the writer producing volume without value.

AI does not solve this problem. AI makes this problem more visible. AI reveals who was writing and who was merely generating.

Kevin was merely generating.

Kevin is now being out generated.

But the writers who were writing, who were judging, who were applying human discernment to human experience and producing prose that contained presence, those writers are still necessary.

Those writers are more necessary than ever. Those writers are the only ones who can do what AI cannot: mean something.

If you can mean something, AI is a tool. If you cannot, AI is a replacement.

Kevin cannot mean something. Kevin is being replaced. Kevin deserves to be replaced.

Not because Kevin is bad. Because Kevin was never

doing the thing that mattered. Kevin was doing the thing that could be automated, and now it has been automated, and Kevin's obsolescence is not tragedy but correction.

The market always needed judgment more than generation. The market just did not have a cheap source of generation to make this clear.

Now it does.

The writers with judgment remain.

The writers without it are exposed.

Kevin is exposed.

Give an AI nothing. No prompt. No style guide. No samples of your work. Let it generate uncued, generic output.

If that output is indistinguishable from yours, the problem is not the machine.

You are the machine.

You have been the machine.

The machine just arrived cheaper.

The AI did not ruin Kevin.

The AI revealed Kevin.


***Tools change.***
***Judgment never becomes measurable.***

# CHAPTER ELEVEN
## AUTHORITY WITHOUT EXPOSURE

**The loudest voices often have the quietest resumes.**

KEVIN IS AN EXPERT.

Kevin has opinions about craft. Kevin has theories about the industry. Kevin has advice for other writers, freely given, frequently shared, always delivered with the confidence of someone who has been there and learned the lessons.

Kevin has never published a book that sold.

**This is Authority Without Exposure.**

This is the peculiar phenomenon of people who speak with certainty about domains they have never successfully navigated. Kevin knows how to write a bestseller. Kevin knows how to query agents. Kevin knows how to build a platform. Kevin knows all of this without ever having done any of it successfully, and the absence of success does not diminish Kevin's confidence.

If anything, it increases it.

Kevin has time to develop theories precisely because Kevin is not busy succeeding. Kevin can spend hours analyzing the industry precisely because the industry has not welcomed Kevin in. Kevin can accumulate knowledge about craft precisely because Kevin is not occupied with the messy business of actually making things that work.

**Knowledge is not authority.**

Reading about surgery does not make you a surgeon. Watching cooking shows does not make you a chef. Studying the market does not make you a successful participant in it. There is a gap between knowing and doing, and the gap can only be crossed by doing.

Kevin has not crossed the gap. Kevin is standing on the knowing side, shouting advice across to people who are trying to cross, and some of those people are listening because Kevin sounds confident and confidence is convincing.

**This is how Kevin Culture reproduces.**

Kevin teaches other Kevins. Kevin leads workshops for aspiring writers who do not know that Kevin has never succeeded. Kevin writes blog posts about the craft of writing that are read by people who assume Kevin must have accomplished something to speak so authoritatively. Kevin builds a following of people who want to learn, and Kevin teaches them what Kevin knows, which is everything except how to actually succeed.

The teaching feels like achievement. The authority feels like accomplishment.

Kevin is doing something. Kevin is contributing. Kevin is helping others navigate the path, and the fact that Kevin has never reached the destination is a detail, a technicality, an irrelevance in the larger project of sharing what Kevin has learned.

But what has Kevin learned? Kevin has learned how to talk about writing. Kevin has not learned how to write in a way that holds strangers.

These are different skills.

The skill of talking about writing is abundant. The skill of analyzing craft, identifying techniques, explaining structures is common. This skill can be developed by reading books about writing, by attending workshops, by participating in online communities where craft is discussed endlessly. This skill requires no publication, no sales, no external validation. This skill can be cultivated in complete isolation from the market.

**The skill of writing that holds is rare.**

The skill of writing that holds requires doing it, failing, revising, failing differently, revising again, submitting to judgment, receiving feedback, integrating feedback, and repeating until something works. This skill cannot be developed in theory. This skill can only be developed in practice, in the uncomfortable zone where your work is evaluated by people who have no reason to be kind.

Kevin avoids this zone.

Kevin has substituted authority for exposure.

Exposure means putting your work in front of people who can reject it. Exposure means risking the verdict. Exposure means discovering that your theories about craft do not translate into prose that functions.

Authority requires no exposure.

Authority can be accumulated in safety. Authority can be built through speaking, teaching, advising, all without ever submitting to the judgment that would reveal whether the authority is earned.

Kevin has accumulated enormous authority. Kevin has submitted to almost no exposure. The gap between these two is the measure of Kevin's self deception.

Watch for the signs.

The writer who talks more than they write. The teacher who has never published in the genre they teach. The advisor whose credits are thin or old or irrelevant. The expert whose expertise is in the meta level, the industry analysis, the craft discussion, never in the actual making of things that succeed.

These people are not necessarily lying.

These people may genuinely believe they have authority. They have studied, after all. They have learned. They have accumulated knowledge that feels substantial because it is extensive.

But knowledge without application is untested. Knowledge without application is theory. Theory without practice is speculation dressed as wisdom.

Kevin is speculating. Kevin has been speculating for years. Kevin has built an entire identity on speculation, and the identity is convincing because Kevin believes it, and belief is contagious.

This is how Kevin harms others.

Kevin's authority attracts people who want to learn. These people trust Kevin because Kevin speaks with confidence. These people follow Kevin's advice because Kevin seems to know things. These people spend time, money, and energy implementing strategies that Kevin has never tested, following paths that Kevin has never walked.

When they fail, Kevin has explanations.

The market has changed. The timing was wrong. The execution was flawed. Kevin's advice was sound; the implementation was the problem. Kevin remains authoritative. Kevin's students absorb the blame for outcomes that Kevin's untested theories produced.

This cycle can continue indefinitely. Kevin never runs out of advice. Kevin's students never stop failing. The connection between these two facts is never examined.

The way out is simple.

**Ask for credentials.**

Not credentials in the sense of degrees or certifications. Credentials in the sense of outcomes. What has this person done? What have they published? Did it succeed? Can you verify the success? Is the success in a domain relevant to what they are teaching?

- The person teaching you how to query agents: have they successfully queried agents? Have they gotten representation? Have they sold books?
- The person teaching you how to self publish: have they self published successfully? Do their books sell? Can you verify the sales numbers?
- The person teaching you craft: do their books demonstrate the craft they preach? Are those books good? Do they hold?

These questions feel rude. These questions feel like you are challenging someone's authority.

You are.

**Challenge it.**

Authority that cannot survive challenge was not authority. Authority that collapses under questioning was speculation. Authority that retreats into offense when credentials are requested was never earned.

The writer who has done the thing will show you. The writer who has succeeded will have evidence. The writer who has submitted to exposure and survived will not be threatened by your request for proof.

Kevin will be threatened.

Kevin will explain why credentials do not matter. Kevin will argue that success is not the only measure. Kevin will suggest that your request for evidence is itself a kind of gatekeeping, an elitist demand that excludes voices who have valuable perspectives regardless of commercial outcomes.

This argument is seductive.

This argument is wrong.

Commercial outcomes are not the only measure of value. Writing can be meaningful without selling. Teaching can be valuable without the teacher having succeeded in the market.

But there is a difference between teaching what you know and teaching what you imagine. There is a difference between sharing experience and sharing theory. There is a difference between authority earned through exposure and authority accumulated through avoidance.

Kevin has accumulated. Kevin has not earned. Kevin's students pay the price.

The saddest part is that Kevin often does not know.

Kevin genuinely believes the authority is real. Kevin has spent so much time studying, analyzing, thinking about writing that the knowledge feels substantial. Kevin has surrounded himself with people who treat the authority as real. Kevin has built a reality in which the gap between knowing and doing has been erased.

Kevin is not malicious. Kevin is deluded. The delusion harms.

The delusion harms Kevin, who never confronts the gap. The delusion harms Kevin's students, who trust advice that has never been tested. The delusion harms the broader culture, which fills with voices speaking confidently about things they have never done.

The solution is exposure. Not for Kevin's students. For Kevin.

Kevin needs to submit to the market. Kevin needs to write the book, finish the book, publish the book, and discover whether Kevin's theories survive contact with reality. Kevin needs to experience what it feels like to have strangers judge work that Kevin made, not work that Kevin analyzed.

This will be painful. This will reveal the gap.

The gap will either be smaller than Kevin feared, in which case Kevin's authority gains foundation, or larger than Kevin admitted, in which case Kevin's authority was always hollow.

Either outcome is better than the current state. Either outcome replaces speculation with knowledge. Either outcome converts authority without exposure into something real.

Kevin resists this. Kevin prefers the safety of theory. Kevin will continue accumulating authority that has never been tested, teaching lessons that have never been learned, advising paths that have never been walked.

Do not follow Kevin. Find the writers who have done it. Find the teachers who have the scars. Find the advisors who can point to outcomes, not opinions.

Those people have paid for their authority with exposure.

Their authority is worth something.

Kevin's is not.

**If you sell directions to a place you have never been, you are not a guide. You are running a con.**

# CHAPTER TWELVE
## SANCTIONED ENDINGS

**A dead dream makes excellent fertilizer.**

SOME DREAMS DESERVE TO DIE.

This is not cruelty.

This is mercy.

The dream that has calcified into identity, the dream that consumes without producing, the dream that demands protection from reality, that dream is not a dream anymore. That dream is a tumor. It grows by feeding on the tissue around it: time, money, relationships, sanity, the finite hours of a finite life spent defending something that will never arrive.

That dream needs to die. Not because the dreamer is

worthless. Because the dreamer is worth more than the dream.

Kevin cannot hear this.

Kevin has merged so completely with the dream that killing the dream feels like killing the self. Kevin has organized an entire identity around being a writer, being someone who is working on a book, being someone whose real life will begin when the book succeeds.

The dream is not something Kevin *has*. The dream is something Kevin *is*.

This is the trap. When the dream becomes identity, the dream becomes unkillable. Every threat to the dream is a threat to the self.

There is a word Kevin uses when all other defenses fail: **Calling.**

*"I was called to write." "This is my purpose." "God gave me this story." "I cannot stop because stopping would be betraying who I am."*

Calling is the final fortress. Calling cannot be argued with. Calling comes from somewhere higher than the market, older than the industry, deeper than craft. Calling is sacred, and sacred things cannot be questioned without committing sacrilege.

This is how calling becomes a cage.

Meaning scarcity creates the trap.

When writing is the only thing that makes your life feel significant, when the book is the only structure holding your identity together, when the dream is the last place where you are special, then questioning the dream feels like annihilation.

You cannot examine it. You cannot test it. You can only protect it.

But a calling that cannot be examined is not discernment. It is fixation.

A calling that requires ignoring reality to survive is not a calling. It is a coping structure.

There is a difference between being called to write and being called to publish. There is a difference between being called to create and being called to sell. Writing may be your calling. Selling books may not be. The two are not the same vocation, and conflating them is how people spend decades defending a dream that was never the right shape.

Calling can function as a deferral mechanism. As long as you are "following your calling," you do not have to examine whether the calling is producing anything that holds. As long as God told you to write, the market's silence is just a test of faith. As long as the purpose is sacred, the results are irrelevant.

This is not faithfulness.

Faithfulness is not sameness. Faithfulness is responsiveness. Faithfulness listens. Faithfulness adapts. Faithfulness asks what the call looks like now, given what reality has already said. Faithfulness does not cement itself into a single form and call the cement holy.

The question is not *"Did God tell you to write?"* The question is *"What would listening look like now, given what reality has already said?"*

If reality has said, for years, that strangers do not want this book, then listening might mean writing a different book. Or writing for a different audience. Or writing for no audience at all, just for the act, just for the survival, just for the getting it out.

Or it might mean stopping.

Stopping is not betrayal.

**Stopping might be the most faithful thing you ever do.**

Stopping might be the moment you finally hear what the call was actually saying, underneath all the noise you layered on top of it.

The call was never "be famous." The call was never "sell books." The call was never "prove everyone wrong."

The call, if it was real, was something simpler. Something that does not require an audience. Something that does not require a market. Something that survives even if no stranger ever reads a word.

If you cannot find that thing underneath the ambition, the calling was not a calling. It was a costume. And costumes do not survive the lion.

Every suggestion that the dream might not be achievable is an attack on the dreamer's core. The dream has wrapped itself around the ego so tightly that they cannot be separated without surgery.

**The surgery is called quitting.**

Quitting is not failure.

Quitting is decision.

Quitting is the recognition that the resources being spent on this pursuit could be spent elsewhere, that the years remaining are finite, that the return on investment has been calculated and found negative.

Quitting is intelligence.

Kevin cannot quit.

Kevin has been told, since childhood, that quitting is weakness. Kevin has absorbed the cultural mythology of persistence: never give up, keep going, success is just around the corner, the breakthrough happens right after you wanted to stop. Kevin has internalized a story in which quitting is the one unforgivable sin.

The story is wrong.

The story was invented by people selling persistence. The story serves those who profit from Kevin continuing: the workshop leaders, the writing coaches, the vanity publishers, the whole ecosystem that extracts money from hope. The story keeps Kevin paying, keeps Kevin trying, keeps Kevin feeding the machine that feeds on Kevins.

The story does not serve Kevin.

Kevin would be better served by the truth.

The truth is that most people who want to write books will not write books that succeed. The truth is that effort does not guarantee outcome. The truth is that years can be spent on pursuits that lead nowhere, and those years do not come back, and the only way to stop losing years is to stop.

**The truth is that quitting is sometimes the right move.** Not always. Not easily. Not without grief.

Kevin is afraid of grief.

Kevin has been avoiding grief for years by avoiding the ending. As long as the dream continues, as long as Someday remains possible, as long as the next book or the next query or the next platform might be the one that works, Kevin does not have to grieve. Kevin can stay in the liminal space between trying and failing, the space where hope is maintained by refusing to test it.

This space is comfortable.

This space is death.

This space is where Kevin will spend the remaining years, neither succeeding nor stopping, neither arriving nor departing, suspended in the amber of perpetual almost.

The grief is necessary. The grief is what allows movement.

The grief says: *this dream is over. This version of the future is not coming. The person I thought I would become, the published author, the successful writer, the vindicated artist, that person is not me. That person was a possibility, and the possibility has closed, and now I must become someone else.*

This hurts. This hurts more than Kevin can imagine, which is why Kevin has been avoiding it.

But on the other side of the hurt is freedom.

On the other side of the hurt is time reclaimed. Energy redirected. Attention freed. The resources that were being poured into the dream can now be poured elsewhere, into pursuits that might actually yield, into relationships that have been neglected, into parts of the self that have been starved.

On the other side of the hurt is a life that is no longer on hold.

On the other side of the hurt, the silence that sounded like failure sounds like the first breath after too long underwater.

But only on the other side.

Kevin's life has been on hold for years. Kevin has been waiting. Waiting for the book to succeed. Waiting for the world to recognize. Waiting for the real life to begin, the life that starts after the dream comes true.

The dream is not coming true. The real life is the only life. The waiting is the waste.

Ending the dream ends the waiting. Ending the dream starts the living.

This is what Kevin cannot see. Kevin thinks that ending

the dream is the end of everything. Kevin thinks that without the identity of writer, there is no identity at all. Kevin has so thoroughly confused the aspiration with the self that removing the aspiration feels like annihilation.

It is not annihilation.

**It is amputation.**

Amputation hurts.

Amputation leaves a wound.

Amputation requires recovery, adaptation, the learning of new ways to move through the world.

Amputation also saves lives.

The limb that is gangrenous, that is poisoning the body, that will kill the whole organism if left attached, that limb must go. The surgeon who removes it is not cruel. The surgeon is preserving what can be preserved by sacrificing what must be sacrificed.

The dream has become gangrenous. The dream is poisoning Kevin's life. The dream must go.

This is not giving up.

Giving up implies that success was possible and was abandoned. That framing assumes that the dream was achievable, that Kevin could have made it if Kevin had just tried harder, that the failure is in the stopping rather than in the starting.

This framing is wrong. Some dreams were never achievable.

Some dreams were mismatched from the beginning: the dreamer's capacity and the dream's requirements were never aligned. Some dreams were predicated on fantasy, on a misunderstanding of what success requires, on the false belief that wanting is enough.

Ending those dreams is not giving up. Ending those dreams is waking up.

The dreamer who wakes up has not failed. The dreamer who wakes up has succeeded at something harder than achieving the dream: they have achieved clarity. They have looked at reality without flinching. They have weighed the evidence and rendered a verdict. They have done what Kevin cannot do, which is to tell themselves the truth.

**The truth is heavy.**

The truth is also liberating.

The writer who decides to stop writing has made a decision. The decision may be painful, but it is a decision, and decisions are power. The decision says: *I am in control of this. I am choosing this. I am not a victim of circumstance; I am an agent who has evaluated the situation and chosen a path.*

Kevin is not in control.

Kevin is being carried by the dream. The dream makes the decisions. The dream determines how Kevin spends time, money, energy. Kevin is a passenger in a vehicle that is driving in circles, never arriving, burning fuel, going nowhere.

Taking the wheel requires ending the ride. Taking the wheel requires saying: *this is over now. I am going somewhere else.*

There are only two sanctioned endings.

## 1. The Artifact That Holds

The dream ends when the dream comes true. You finish the book. The book works. Strangers read it and are held. The market notices. The verdict arrives, and the verdict is yes. The dream has been achieved. The dream can end because it has been realized.

This ending is available to some people.

This ending requires that the dreamer had the capacity, did the work, produced something that functions. This ending is not available to everyone because capacity is not evenly distributed and effort does not guarantee outcome.

If this ending is available to you, pursue it. Finish the book. Make it work. Submit it to judgment. See what happens.

## 2. The Burial

The dream ends when you decide it ends. You stop. You grieve. You bury the dream in a grave marked with the years you spent on it, the pages you wrote, the hope you carried. You say goodbye. You walk away.

This ending is available to everyone.

This ending requires only decision. You do not need capacity. You do not need market approval. You do not need external validation. You need only the willingness to let go.

Letting go is not weakness. Letting go is the hardest thing Kevin will ever do.

Kevin has been holding on for so long that letting go feels like falling. Kevin does not know who Kevin is without the dream. Kevin does not know what to do with the hours that were filled by hoping. Kevin does not know how to answer the question "What do you do?" without saying "I'm a writer."

Kevin will have to learn. Kevin will have to become someone new. Kevin will have to grieve the person Kevin thought Kevin would be and become the person Kevin actually is.

This is terrifying. This is also the door.

The only way out of Kevin is through the ending. The endless middle, the perpetual almost, the Someday that never arrives, that is not a life. That is a holding pattern.

That is a waiting room where Kevin sits while the years tick by, waiting for a name that will never be called.

Stop waiting.

Choose an ending.

Either finish the book and submit it to judgment, or stop and submit yourself to grief. Both are better than the middle. Both are better than the waiting. Both are doors that lead somewhere, even if the somewhere is painful, even if the somewhere is not what you wanted.

The middle leads nowhere.

Kevin is in the middle. Kevin has been in the middle for years. Kevin will die in the middle if Kevin does not choose.

**Choose.**

The dream dies unburied or buried. Silence follows either way. But only one silence is peace.

The middle is not free. Others are funding it. Their time, their money, their rationed patience. Refusing to choose is a choice. The people who love you have been paying for it.


*Hope is the saddest drug when it's stapled to the wrong dream.*

# CHAPTER THIRTEEN
## KEVIN, STOP READING THIS CHAPTER

**Your persistence is their fatigue.**

KEVIN, **this chapter is not for you.**

Close the book.

You were warned in the beginning. You were told this would happen. You were given every opportunity to recognize yourself and turn back. You did not turn back. You kept reading, convinced that you were different, that the diagnosis did not apply, that somewhere in these pages you would find the exception that proved you were not Kevin after all.

There is no exception. You are Kevin. And this chapter is not for you.

This chapter is for the people you have exhausted.

The people who smile when you talk about your book because not smiling makes you difficult. The people who nod when you explain why the industry is broken because arguing takes more energy than they have left. The people downstream of your dream, drowning in the flood of your need.

Kevin, stop reading.

You will not stop. You never stop. That is the problem. You do not know when to stop talking, stop explaining, stop demanding that others participate in your fantasy. You will read this chapter looking for ammunition, looking for evidence that you are being persecuted, looking for proof that this book is just another gatekeeper trying to keep you out.

Fine. Read it. But know that every word from here forward is aimed past you, at the people standing behind you, the people you cannot see because you have never turned around to look.


## TO THE EDITORS

You know the query before you open it.

The subject line is too long. The greeting is too familiar. The pitch is not a pitch but a confession, a life story, a justification for why this manuscript matters that has nothing to do with whether the manuscript works.

You read the first paragraph anyway. The prose is not ready. The prose may never be ready. The person who wrote it does not know this, and telling them will cost you something you cannot afford to spend.

So you send the form rejection or you send nothing at all. You delete the email and move to the next one, knowing there will be another just like it, and another, and another. An endless parade of Kevins who believe you are the obstacle between them and the success they deserve.

You are not the obstacle.

The prose is the obstacle.

But you cannot say that. Saying it invites argument. Saying it opens a conversation you do not have time for with a person who is not listening.

Your silence is not cruelty.

Your silence is survival.

The volume is not manageable. The ratio of viable to dead is not sustainable. You are doing triage in a disaster zone. Most of what comes through the door is already a corpse. You cannot resuscitate it. You cannot explain to it why it died. You can only tag it and move on.

Kevin does not understand this.

Kevin thinks you did not read carefully. Kevin thinks you missed something. Kevin thinks that if you had only given the manuscript a real chance, you would have seen what Kevin sees. Kevin is wrong.

You saw plenty. You saw enough. You saw in seconds what Kevin cannot see after years: that this is not ready, and the person who made it does not know how to make it ready.

Your exhaustion is valid.

Your silence is data.

Keep the arteries clear.

. . .

## TO THE LIBRARIANS

You see them coming.

There is a posture. A gait. A brightness in the eyes that signals what is about to happen. Someone is approaching the desk with a book. *Their* book. A book they wrote, they published, and now need you to validate by placing on your shelves.

The book is self published. The cover is wrong. The spine does not have correct information. The interior formatting is amateur. The price is too high for what it is. You know before you open it that the prose inside will match the presentation outside.

But you are kind. You are kind because kindness is your nature and because your institution values community engagement and because this person is a patron, a neighbor, a member of the public you serve.

So you smile. You take the book. You say you will consider it. You do not say that your acquisition budget is limited, your shelf space is finite, your professional judgment tells you this book will not circulate because it is not good enough to circulate.

You add it to the pile.

The pile is large. The pile is the accumulated dreams of every Kevin in your community. Every person who believed that writing a book entitled them to shelf space. Every local author who conflated production with quality.

You feel guilty about the pile. You should not feel guilty.

The pile is not your failure. The pile is the failure of a culture that told people writing a book was enough, that did not explain the difference between making something and making something good, that handed participation trophies to everyone who crossed the starting line regardless of whether they finished the race.

You are not a gatekeeper.

You are a curator.

Your job is to connect readers with books they will value. Your job is not to validate every person who wants to be valued. Your job requires judgment, and judgment requires saying no, and saying no to Kevins is exhausting because Kevins do not hear no.

They hear: *try harder.* They hear: *convince me.* They hear: *this is a negotiation.*

It is not a negotiation.

It is a verdict.

The verdict is not cruelty. The verdict is your professional assessment that this book will not serve your readers.

Trust the verdict.

## TO THE FAMILIES

You did not sign up for this.

You fell in love with a person, not a dream. You married a partner, not a protagonist in a story that never ends. You wanted a life together. You got a life on hold. A life waiting. A life organized around something that was always about to happen and never did.

You have been supportive. You have been so supportive.

You have listened to the plot summaries, the character descriptions, the industry complaints. You have nodded through the explanations of why this agent did not understand, why that publisher was wrong, why the market is broken in ways that specifically disadvantage your spouse.

You have paid.

You have paid in money, in time, in attention, in the slow erosion of your own needs to make room for the dream that swallowed your household.

You have said "It's good" when you did not know if it was good. You do not know how to evaluate it. Saying anything else would start a fight you do not have the energy to finish.

Your praise was kindness.

Your kindness was damage.

It is not your fault. You were doing what love does: supporting, encouraging, believing. You were being a good partner to someone who needed you to believe in them. How could you know that your belief was insulation, that your support was scaffolding for a structure that would never stand on its own?

You could not know.

You were not trained to evaluate prose. You were trained to love, and you loved, and the love kept the dream alive past the point where the dream should have been examined.

This is not your guilt to carry. But it might be your intervention to make.

**Someone has to say it.**

Someone has to say: *this is not working. This has not been working for years. The book is not coming together. The agents are not wrong. The market is not broken. The dream has become a weight we are both carrying.*

*I cannot carry it anymore.*

Someone has to ask for pages.

Not praise of pages. Pages. Actual pages that can be read and evaluated. Someone has to demand the artifact rather than accepting the intention. Someone has to say: *show me what you have made, and I will tell you what I see, even if what I see is not what you want me to see.*

This is not betrayal. This is love that has stopped lying.

Love that lies is not love. It is comfort. Comfort feels good in the moment and costs everything over time. Comfort enables the dream to grow past the point of sustainability, to consume resources that were meant for the life you were building together.

You are allowed to stop providing comfort. You are allowed to ask questions. You are allowed to say: *I need to know if this is going anywhere, because my life is going somewhere, with or without this dream.*

That conversation will be painful.

That conversation might save both of you.


## TO EVERYONE DOWNSTREAM OF KEVIN

You did not fail Kevin.

Kevin failed the artifact.

Kevin had years to produce something that worked. Kevin had access to feedback, to craft resources, to the same information available to everyone who succeeds. Kevin chose not to use them. Or used them and did not improve. Or improved and still did not reach the threshold where strangers would care.

That is not your fault.

You cannot want it for them harder than they are willing to work for it. You cannot carry a dream that the dreamer has not built strong enough to bear its own weight. You cannot save someone who is not drowning but floating, happily, in the delusion that floating is swimming.

Your exhaustion is valid.

Your boundaries are necessary.

Your silence is not cruelty.

It is the only honest verdict left when words have failed, when explanation has been rejected, when every attempt to communicate reality has been absorbed into the narrative of persecution.

The system is not broken.

The system is clogged.

You are standing in the clog.

**Kevin is the clog.**

When you stop feeding Kevin, when you stop providing the reassurance that keeps the dream inflated, when you allow the silence to speak, you are not being cruel.

You are being clear.

Clarity is what Kevin needs. Clarity is what Kevin will not accept from you, but that does not make it wrong to offer.

Stop feeding them.

Every time you say "keep going" to someone who is not finishing, you make finishing rarer for everyone else. Every time you praise work that does not function, you delay the reckoning that might actually help. Every time you absorb the weight of someone else's dream, you have less capacity for your own life.

Stop absorbing.

Let the dream carry its own weight.

If it falls, it was not strong enough.

If it stands, your honesty did not kill it.

Either way, you are free.

Kevin, if you are still reading, the diagnosis is complete.

You were warned. You did not stop. You consumed even this chapter, the chapter that was explicitly not for you, because consumption is what you do. You take without producing. You demand without delivering. You read even the words that name your pattern because you cannot stop yourself from believing that the next word might be the one that exempts you.

There is no exemption. There is only the choice.

Finish the book and submit it to strangers. Or stop and grieve and become someone else.

The people in your life are tired. The people in your life deserve to stop waiting. The people in your life are not your audience, your validators, your support system for a dream that has become a demand.

Let them go.

Let the dream go.

Or make the dream real by doing the work.

Those are the only options.

The middle is where everyone suffers.

The rest of us have work to do.


***Kevin does not just waste his own time.***
***He wastes everyone else's.***

# CHAPTER FOURTEEN
## THE LION IS WAITING

**Silence is the only applause that matters.**

## YOU ARE STILL HERE.

After everything.

After the chapter that told you to stop.

After the chapters that named your pattern.

After the ladder that mapped your descent.

After the diagnosis, that left no place to hide.

You are still here.

I do not know why.

Maybe you are a Kevin who has read this far because Kevins cannot stop consuming, cannot stop seeking the exemption that does not exist, cannot stop believing that somewhere in the text is a loophole that will let them continue as they were.

There is no loophole.

Maybe you are not a Kevin.

Maybe you recognized pieces of yourself in these pages, but also recognized the distance between where you are and where Kevin lives.

Maybe you are someone who needed to see the pattern named so you could avoid it, catch yourself before the descent, and choose differently.

If so, choose.

**Choose now.**

The book is almost over.

The words are almost spent.

Whatever you are going to do with what you have read, you are going to do it soon, in the silence that follows the last page, in the space where the author's voice stops and your own decisions begin.

I will not be there.

I will not follow you into that silence.

I will not check on your progress.

I will not ask how the book is coming.

I will not provide encouragement, accountability, support, or any of the other words that have been weaponized into permission to continue without producing.

**You were always alone with this.**

The writing groups, the online communities, the followers, the family, the friends who said they believed in you, they were company, not help.

They were warmth, not work.

They were the pleasant feeling of being surrounded while you avoided the thing that can only be done in solitude.

The thing that matters is solitary.

The thing that matters is you, in a room, with a manuscript, making decisions.

What to keep.

What to cut.

What to revise.

What to abandon.

These decisions cannot be crowdsourced.

These decisions cannot be delegated.

These decisions are yours, and they will determine whether the artifact holds.

If you are Kevin, you will not make these decisions.

You will close this book and return to the pattern.

You will post about how harsh it was, how unfair it was, and how it did not understand your particular situation.

You will gather sympathy from other Kevins who also felt attacked, and the sympathy will feel like vindication, and the vindication will feel like permission.

Permission to continue as you were.

Permission to keep announcing without finishing.

Permission to keep descending the ladder, rung by rung, toward the bottom where the bitter **Theft Kevin** lives, blaming everyone but himself for everything that went wrong.

If that is your choice, make it.

Make it clearly.

Make it knowing what you are choosing.

Do not pretend you did not know.

Do not claim, years from now, that no one told you.

Do not say you were never warned.

This book is a warning.

This chapter is a warning.

Every page has been a warning.

You have been warned.

**The lion is still waiting.**

The lion has been waiting since before the first chapter.

The lion will wait forever because it is patient and does not need you.

The lion has plenty to eat.

The lion is not specifically hungry for your book.

The lion is simply there, in the clearing where verdicts happen, doing what lions do.

If you enter the clearing, the lion will judge you.

The lion will decide, based on the artifact you present, whether to eat it or let it live.

The lion will make this decision quickly, without mercy, without considering how hard you worked or how much you sacrificed or how badly you wanted a different outcome.

The lion is not cruel.

The lion is not kind.

The lion is just the lion, and the lion's judgment is the only judgment that matters.

Kevin never enters the clearing.

Kevin stays at the edge, talking about the lion, analyzing the lion, explaining why the lion is unfair, gathering with other edge dwellers who also have theories about what the lion wants and why the lion is wrong to want it.

The edge dwellers never find out.

The edge dwellers grow old at the edge, still talking, still theorizing, still believing that their understanding of the lion substitutes for the experience of facing it.

It does not substitute.

Nothing substitutes.

The only way to know if your work holds is to present it to the lion.

The only way to know if you are a writer is to write something that survives judgment.

The only way out of Kevin is through the clearing.

If you are Kevin, leave.

**Leave now.**

Go back to the edge of the clearing where it is safe.

Go back to the writing groups and the online communities and the endless conversations about craft that never produce craft.

Go back to the comfortable fantasy where you are almost a writer, almost there, almost ready.

**Stay almost.**

**Die almost.**

Be buried with your almost book and your almost career and your almost life that never quite began because you were always preparing for a moment you never let arrive.

That is your right.

That is your choice.

Make it and go.

If you are not Kevin, or if you refuse to remain Kevin, then there is nothing left to say.

You know what to do.

You have always known.

The only question was whether you would do it.

Answer the question.

Not with words.

With work!

**Does this hold a stranger?**

Not does it hold your mother.

Not does it hold your writing group.

Not does it hold the version of you that needed to believe it was good.

**Does it hold a stranger who owes you nothing?**

If yes, finish it.

Ship it.

Let the lion decide.

If no, bury it.

**Grieve it.**

**Become someone else.**

Both of these are endings.

Both of these are survival.

Everything else is the middle, and the middle is where Kevin lives, and Kevin lives there forever, and forever smells like decay.

You finished.

Not the book.

This book.

The one in your hands.

The one that has been burning down the walls you built around yourself for the last hundred pages.

You survived.

That is all you get.

No instructions.

No next steps.

No resources.

No community to join.

No newsletter to subscribe to.

No coaching program that will fix what this book broke. **You are standing in the wreckage, and no one is coming to help you sort through it.**

If you finished this book and feel lighter, something that needed to die has died.

Do not try to resuscitate it.

Do not go back to the writing group tomorrow and explain what you learned.

Do not post about your "breakthrough."

The thing that died was feeding on your attention.

Starve the corpse.

If you finished this book and feel angry, good.

Anger means something has lost its protection.

Anger means a wall came down.

Anger means you are not numb.

What you do with the anger is your problem.

You can use it to prove me wrong by finishing something that holds.

You can use it to finally bury the thing you have been dragging around for years.

You can use it to hate me forever while quietly knowing I was right.

I do not care which one you choose.

If you finished this book and feel nothing, you were never Kevin.

You were a tourist.

You came to watch the fire.

You can leave now.

The exits are clearly marked.

If you finished this book and feel sick, if your hands are shaking, if you want to call someone and explain why this book is unfair, if you are already composing the rebuttal in your head, if you are telling yourself that your situation is different, that your book is different, that your pain is different, that your dream is different.

**Stop.**

That feeling is the diagnosis landing.

That feeling is the pattern recognizing itself.

That feeling is the last wall coming down, and you are standing in the open, and the lion is right there, and there is nowhere left to hide.

You have two choices.

You can rebuild the walls.

You can find a softer book.

You can return to the Collective.

You can tell yourself this was just one person's opinion, just one harsh voice in a chorus of encouragement, just noise to be filtered out on the way back to Someday.

You can do that.

Most people will.

Or you can stand in the open.

Someday is a lie you tell the calendar.

**If the dream was wrong, the hope was a lie, and the lie was expensive, and the expense was your life.**

You do not get the years back.

You only get the years that remain.

If you stop, stopping is not the end of anything.

It is a different beginning.

You are alone with this.

You were always alone with this.

The difference is that now you know it.

The pretending is over.

The lion is waiting.

The silence is coming.

It comes for everyone.

The only question is whether it finds you mid sentence or mid excuse.


**_Now get out of my sight._**
    **_I've got real sins to commit._**

# ABOUT THE AUTHOR

Coyote Gray Jr published Stay and thought that would be the end of it. Then he started noticing Kevin. Kevin at the coffee shop, Kevin in the writing group, Kevin in the feed, Kevin in the mirror on the bad mornings. The book that resulted is not kind, which is the point. He runs a ranch in central New Mexico, holds a philosophy degree from UNM, and has read and seen too much since. He did not consult anyone before writing this. The people who would have told him not to are the people the book is about. The lion remains unfed and uninterested in his feelings on the matter.

For permissions, inquiries, or correspondence:
Coyote Pack Publishing
info@coyotepackpublishing.com